# Preparation for Total Consecration to the Holy Face of Jesus

# Preparation for Total Consecration to the

# Holy Face of Jesus

## How God Draws the Soul through the Purgative, Illuminative, and Unitive Ways

Father Lawrence Daniel Carney III

TAN Books
Gastonia, North Carolina

In accord with canon 827 of the Code of Canon Law, I hereby grant my approval (or permission) to publish *Preparation for Consecration to the Holy Face*, by Fr. Lawrence Carney III.

Bishop Carl A. Kemme
Bishop of Wichita April 11, 2025

Nihil Obstat: Fr. Thomas Hoisington, S.T.L.
Censor Librorum
April 11, 2025

Imprimatur: ✠ Bishop Carl A. Kemme
Bishop of Wichita
April 11, 2025



Unless otherwise noted, Scripture quotations are from the Douay-Rheims Bible.

A special thanks to the Bishop Sheen Today apostolate for permission to use The Little Chaplet of the Holy Face graphic.

Cover design by Jordan Avery

Cover image: Jesus Christ the Savior. Shutterstock/only_vector.

Interior Image: Provided by Congregation of the Sons of the Most Holy Redeemer, Papa Stronsay, UK.

ISBN: 978-1-5051-3485-8
Kindle ISBN: 978-1-5051-3731-6
ePUB ISBN: 978-1-5051-3730-9

Published in the United States by
TAN Books
PO Box 269
Gastonia, NC 28053
www.TANBooks.com
Printed in India

*To the Holy Face of Jesus, who looked upon St. Peter after his denial with a look of love that wounded him and who wounds with love all wretched sinners who are trying to follow the Good Shepherd.*

*"Fáciem meam non avérti ab increpántibus et conspuéntibus in me. Dóminus Deus auxiliátor meus, et ídeo non sum confúsus."*

—Is. 50:6–7

*"I have given my body to the strikers, and my cheeks to them that plucked them: I have not turned away my face from them that rebuked me, and spit upon me. The Lord God is my helper, therefore am I not confounded."*

—Brief Lesson for the Divine Office of Prime during Passiontide

*"Therefore have I set my face as a most hard rock, and I know that I shall not be confounded."*

—Is. 50:7

*"O Lord Jesus, raise up someone who will renew with zeal and love the divine Order of St. Peter, even as St. Dominic has established his in Thy Church."*

—Ven. Mons. Olier Founder of the Sulpicians

# Contents

# Introduction

The word *interference*, when used by exorcists, means possession, obsession, or oppression by the demonic. The world, the flesh, and the devil constantly interfere with each member of the Church Militant by being a hindrance, impediment, or obstacle.

Jesus taught by parables. Some people understood the message, while others remained blind. Why? The blind, in the spiritual sense, missed the point of the parable. They remained in their sin, hardened of heart. But the apostles and disciples of Jesus understood the story. How? They became little.

Saint Matthew records Jesus: "Who thinkest thou is greater in the kingdom of heaven? And Jesus calling unto him a little child, set him in the midst of them, And said, Amen I say to you, unless you be converted, and become as little children, you shall not enter into the kingdom of heaven."[1]

Why does one need to become little today? One must be little in order to understand the parable of today, which is still told by Scripture, Tradition, and private revelation. When one becomes little, God can speak to the heart so it can understand what to do today.

Heaven has spoken to mankind through the prophets, evangelists, and Jesus Christ, our Redeemer. That is known as

1 Matt. 18:1–3.

the deposit of faith, or public revelation. But heaven continues to speak to us, in parable, through private revelation. But care must be taken because there is much interference in the reception of private revelation! In order to receive the message of Our Lady of Fatima and the miracle of the sun, the message to Sr. Marie de St. Pierre in the Archconfraternity of the Holy Face, Our Lady of La Salette, Our Lady of Lourdes, and Our Lady of Revelation, to name a few, the soul must exorcise all interference. Clear understanding of the messages is necessary to recognize the call to live for the triumph of the Sacred Heart, Immaculate Heart, and the Church.

This book is intended to guide the soul on how to live devotion to the Holy Face of Jesus as revealed to Sr. Marie de St. Pierre. It is a follow-up to the previous volume: *The Secret of the Holy Face: The Devotion Destined to Save Society*. That work is the *what* to devotion to the Holy Face. This volume is the *how*. If "reparation is destined to save society,"[2] devotion to the Holy Face, which is the object of reparation, will make our faces "shine with a brightness surpassing that of many others in eternal life."[3] One cannot love what one does not know. Once the soul knows of the greatness of devotion to the Holy Face and is convinced of the need for it in his life, love for the Face of Jesus grows.

The aim of this book is to prepare the soul to see the Face of Jesus, overcoming interference. Now is a critical time for

---

[2] Blessed Pope Pius IX in Janvier, *Life of Sister Mary of St. Peter, Carmel of Tours*, p. 338.

[3] Janvier, *Manual of the Archconfraternity of the Holy Face*, p. 86. From the nine promises of devotion to the Holy Face, which are found in the back of this volume.

this devotion because of today's crical mockery against Christians. It is important now to know the evil of blasphemy and its remedy: reparation to the Holy Face of Jesus. St. Thérèse of the Child Jesus and of the Holy Face, once she lived out this devotion, "saw illusions to the Countenance of the Savior scattered on practically every page of the Psalms of David."[4] Seeing the Face of Jesus through the Archconfraternity of the Holy Face will hopefully aid pagans of good will to desire to enter the Catholic Church, help fallen-away Catholics come back, help lukewarm Catholics become ignited with the fire of the Holy Ghost, and help fervent Catholics overcome the desire to constantly read of the horrible news about the Church and the world and begin to live the life of union with God and grow in the one thing necessary: charity.

The method to achieve the aims of charity and union is the three conversions or ages of the spiritual life as described in the patrimony of spiritual theology: the purgative way, the illuminative way, and the unitive way.[5] The narrative will prepare the soul to make total consecration to the Holy Face of Jesus and to know the value of this consecration. For example, an infant receives baptism, which removes Original Sin. When he reaches the age of reason, he receives instruction on what mortal sin is and how to avoid it, which is the purgative way. Later, he is confirmed, showing that the Holy Ghost strengthens him, and receives an increase of the Gifts of the Holy Ghost, which is the illuminative way. Then one receives Holy Matrimony or enters

---

[4] Scallan, *The Whole World Will Love Me*, p. 199.

[5] Theologians have compared the purgative way to childhood 7–14; the illuminative way to youth 15–20, and the unitive way to adulthood 21–35.

Consecrated Life or Ordination to the priesthood;[6] this could be a symbol of the last age in life, where eventually, as they mature, they will arrive in the unitive way. Or one can see in the journey of the apostles. Jesus calls them to leave their former life and follow Him—the purgative way. They are taught and sent out to preach and heal—the illuminative way. They receive the Holy Ghost at Pentecost—the unitive way. What is clear is that the soul must always be moving toward the unitive way, or its growth will be impeded.

Excerpts from the *Month of the Holy Face*, written by a member of the Priests of the Holy Face,[7] will include biblical devotion to the Holy Face, different scenes of Jesus's Face in the Gospels, and apostles[8] of the Holy Face. The theme of progression through the various stages of the spiritual life is woven through these Holy Face excerpts. Prayers from the Archconfraternity of the Holy Face are included to stir fervor in the soul.

In the current mystical combat, souls of the lay faithful must practice meditation in silence for at least one quarter of an hour.[9] This *minimum*, along with a proper spiritual life, will bring one out of mortal sin and move him beyond into the

---

[6] St. Thomas mentions that growth in charity can be considered to a certain likeness to human growth, i.e., infant, puberty, adult. So, charity grows in degrees, avoiding sin—beginners; secondly, man aims at the progress of good—proficient; and thirdly, man aims for union with God—perfect. *ST* II–II, q. 24, a. 9.

[7] In 1891.

[8] Apostles of the Holy Face are those who have promoted devotion to the Holy Face of Jesus to the faithful in an exceptional way, either by preaching, miracles, or private revelations.

[9] Priests and religious should meditate for at least one hour.

higher regions of the spiritual life.[10] The fruit of the individual spiritual combat can not only save society but also make the greatest saints the world has ever seen. If there is to be a triple triumph (of the Sacred Heart, the Immaculate Heart, and the Catholic Church), would it not include the greatest body of saints? Devotion to the Holy Face is an exalted devotion since the Holy Face represents the divinity of God and is reserved for the saints in the latter times.

If the aims and means of this book are achieved, then faithful readers will not only receive the reward of heaven but will be in her highest mansions! But souls must be small here on earth in order to share copiously in the divine nature. Pick up this book and be little.

The Gospel for the Mass of Saint Michael the Archangel,[11] patron of the Archconfraternity of the Holy Face, taken from the same verses concerning being a little child in Saint Matthew's Gospel, concludes, "for I say to you, that their angels in heaven always see the face of my Father who is in heaven."[12] Also, the Mass of Saint Thérèse of the Holy Face uses the same Gospel (although shorter). Is it providential that Saint Michael, one of the three patrons, and Saint Thérèse, one of the first to enroll in the Archconfraternity of the Holy Face, have this Gospel for their respective Masses concerning being little and always seeing the Face of Jesus's Father? Renounce the world with all its interference and engage in the spiritual life before it is too late.

---

[10] If possible, it is even better to make meditation before the Holy Sacrament of the Altar.

[11] His feast is September 29. Incidentally, the same Gospel selection is used for the Guardian Angels (October 2).

[12] Matt. 18:10.

In conclusion, the soul will profit much if it learns from the ancient rite of infant baptism. The rite calls for three exorcisms: one over salt and two over the infant. This happens before the blessing of the baptism. Note how the demonic is driven from the child before the baptism. The theme applies to the soul. By way of analogy, she must exorcise herself of all interference from the world, the flesh, and the devil before she can receive the blessings of union with God. Thus, the purgative way, rooting out mortal sin, is a prerequisite to the last two stages: the illuminative way and the unitive way.

*"Thou shalt hide them in the secret of thy face,*
*from the disturbance of men."*

—Psalm 30:21

# Daily Exercises

## Seven Suggested Schedules for Consecration

Consecration day with various dates include Shrove Tuesday (Tuesday before Ash Wednesday), Good Friday, and Easter Sunday. Directions: From the consecration day, count from the preceding day backwards thirty-three days. See the following table for: March 25 Annunciation, June 29 St. Peter, July 12, St. Veronica, August 6 Transfiguration, St. Louis August 25, St. Michael September 29, St. Martin of Tours November 11. Other dates: Saint Thérèse, October 3 start August 31; Saints Louis and Zelie Martin, July 12 start June 9 (same as Saint Veronica).

Part 1: (11 Days) Purgative Way—

| | I. | II. | III. |
|---|---|---|---|
| 1st Day | Feb. 20 | May 27 | June 9 |
| 2nd Day | Feb. 21 | May 28 | June 10 |
| 3rd Day | Feb. 22 | May 29 | June 11 |
| 4th Day | Feb. 23 | May 30 | June 12 |
| 5th Day | Feb. 24 | May 31 | June 13 |
| 6th Day | Feb. 25 | June 1 | June 14 |
| 7th Day | Feb. 26 | June 2 | June 15 |
| 8th Day | Feb. 27 | June 3 | June 16 |
| 9th Day | Feb. 28 | June 4 | June 17 |
| 10th Day | March 1 | June 5 | June 18 |
| 11th Day | March 2 | June 6 | June 19 |

Part 2: (11 Days) Illuminative Way of the Proficients—

| | | | |
|---|---|---|---|
| 12th Day | March 3 | June 7 | June 20 |
| 13th Day | March 4 | June 8 | June 21 |
| 14th Day | March 5 | June 9 | June 22 |
| 15th Day | March 6 | June 10 | June 23 |
| 16th Day | March 7 | June 11 | June 24 |
| 17th Day | March 8 | June 12 | June 25 |
| 18th Day | March 9 | June 13 | June 26 |
| 19th Day | March 10 | June 14 | June 27 |
| 20th Day | March 11 | June 15 | June 28 |
| 21st Day | March 12 | June 16 | June 29 |
| 22nd Day | March 13 | June 17 | June 30 |

Part 3: (11 Days) Unitive Way of the Perfect—

| | | | |
|---|---|---|---|
| 23rd Day | March 14 | June 18 | July 1 |
| 24th Day | March 15 | June 19 | July 2 |
| 25th Day | March 16 | June 20 | July 3 |
| 26th Day | March 17 | June 21 | July 4 |
| 27th Day | March 18 | June 22 | July 5 |
| 28th Day | March 19 | June 23 | July 6 |
| 29th Day | March 20 | June 24 | July 7 |
| 30th Day | March 21 | June 25 | July 8 |
| 31st Day | March 22 | June 26 | July 9 |
| 32nd Day | March 23 | June 27 | July 10 |
| 33rd Day | March 24 | June 28 | July 11 |
| Consecration Day | March 25 Annunciation | June 29 St. Peter | July 12 St. Veronica |

Renouncement of the World

| IV. | V. | VI. | VIII. |
|---|---|---|---|
| July 4 | July 23 | Aug. 27 | Oct. 9 |
| July 5 | July 24 | Aug. 28 | Oct. 10 |
| July 6 | July 25 | Aug. 29 | Oct. 11 |
| July 7 | July 26 | Aug. 30 | Oct. 12 |
| July 8 | July 27 | Aug. 31 | Oct. 13 |
| July 9 | July 28 | Sept. 1 | Oct. 14 |
| July 10 | July 29 | Sept. 2 | Oct. 15 |
| July 11 | July 30 | Sept. 3 | Oct. 16 |
| July 12 | July 31 | Sept. 4 | Oct. 17 |
| July 13 | Aug. 1 | Sept. 5 | Oct. 18 |
| July 14 | Aug. 2 | Sept. 6 | Oct. 19 |

Know the Holy Face of Jesus

| | | | |
|---|---|---|---|
| July 15 | Aug. 3 | Sept. 7 | Oct. 20 |
| July 16 | Aug. 4 | Sept. 8 | Oct. 21 |
| July 17 | Aug. 5 | Sept. 9 | Oct. 22 |
| July 18 | Aug. 6 | Sept. 10 | Oct. 23 |
| July 19 | Aug. 7 | Sept. 11 | Oct. 24 |
| July 20 | Aug. 8 | Sept. 12 | Oct. 25 |
| July 21 | Aug. 9 | Sept. 13 | Oct. 26 |
| July 22 | Aug. 10 | Sept. 14 | Oct. 27 |
| July 23 | Aug. 11 | Sept. 15 | Oct. 28 |
| July 24 | Aug. 12 | Sept. 16 | Oct. 29 |
| July 25 | Aug. 13 | Sept. 17 | Oct. 30 |

Heaven Begins to Dwell Within

| | | | |
|---|---|---|---|
| July 26 | Aug. 14 | Sept. 18 | Oct. 31 |
| July 27 | Aug. 15 | Sept. 19 | Nov. 1 |
| July 28 | Aug. 16 | Sept. 20 | Nov. 2 |
| July 29 | Aug. 17 | Sept. 21 | Nov. 3 |
| July 30 | Aug. 18 | Sept. 22 | Nov. 4 |
| July 31 | Aug. 19 | Sept. 23 | Nov. 5 |
| Aug. 1 | Aug. 20 | Sept. 24 | Nov. 6 |
| Aug. 2 | Aug. 21 | Sept. 25 | Nov. 7 |
| Aug. 3 | Aug. 22 | Sept. 26 | Nov. 8 |
| Aug. 4 | Aug. 23 | Sept. 27 | Nov. 9 |
| Aug. 5 | Aug. 24 | Sept. 28 | Nov. 10 |
| Aug. 6<br>Transfiguration | Aug. 25<br>St. Louis, King | Sept. 29<br>St. Michael | Nov. 11<br>St. Martin of Tours |

VERA EFFIGIES SACRI VULTUS D.N. JESU CHRISTI

*quae, Romae, in Sacrosancta Basilica S. Petri in Vaticano religiossime asservatur, et colitur.*

# Practical Suggestions

Baptism is required, and Confirmation is strongly suggested. If one is not going to confession regularly, make a firm commitment to do so before the end of part 1: the purgative way. Mass must be attended every Sunday and on holy days of obligation, but try to attend Mass more often, even daily. It is recommended to make the Total Consecration to Mary before Total Consecration to the Holy Face because it is more humble to approach Jesus through Mary. God gave Jesus through Mary, so it is proper to go to Jesus through Mary.

Enrollment in the Archconfraternity or Confraternity of the Holy Face is optional but worth discernment. There are two consecration prayers: one for members of the (Arch)confraternities and one for non-members.

Get an image of the Holy Face of Jesus. It must be a copy of the Veil of Veronica, not the Shroud of Turin. The former is an object of the Face of the Passion; the latter is the object of His Death. Make a prayer corner or chapel in the house and have a candle or olive oil lamp burning night and day. The warm glow of the light calms the soul in these troubled times. Also, see "Consecration Day (Day 34)" (p. 221) to help you prepare ahead of time.

Become a defender of the Holy Name of God by keeping Holy the Lord's day. Make a commitment to no shopping on

Sunday—make it a day of rest. Consider a family dinner prepared the day in advance. Make an hour of reparation. If blasphemy is heard—memorize the Golden Arrow prayer and say it in reparation. St. Alphonsus Liguori said that blasphemy is one of the worst sins possible.

# Beginning Theme: Purgative Way of Beginners

## Prayers to Be Recited During Each Day of the Purgative Way

### Salutation to Our Lord Jesus Christ

*In Order to Repair the Blasphemies Committed against His Sacred Name*

In union with the whole Church, by the hearts of Mary and of Joseph, all burning with love, and in the name of all men, I salute Thee, I adore Thee, and I love Thee, O Jesus of Nazareth! King of the Jews, full of meekness and of humility, of grace and of truth. Mercy and justice are with Thee; love is Thy substance; Thou art the Christ, the only Son of the living God, and the blessed fruit of the womb of the glorious Virgin Mary.

O Jesus! Good Shepherd, who hast given Thy life for Thy sheep, by all Thy sacred wounds, Thy precious blood, Thy divine tears and beloved sweat, by all the sighs, the groans, the sorrows, the love, the merits of the thirty-three years of Thy holy life, enclosed in the ineffable sanctuary of Thy holy life, have pity on us, poor and miserable sinners; convert all the blasphemers and profaners of the holy day of Sunday, and give us a share in Thy divine merits, now and at the hour of our death. Amen.

## Affectionate Aspirations to Our Lord

### *In Order to Repair the Blasphemies*

O Jesus, eternal truth and wisdom, who wast treated as a seducer and madman, I adore Thee and I love Thee with all my heart.

O Jesus, in whom are all the treasures of divine knowledge, but who wast looked upon as an ignorant man and the son of a carpenter, I adore Thee and I love Thee with all my heart.

O Jesus, fountain of life, who disdst hear the Jews say to Thee: *Will he kill himself*, because Thou saidst to them: *You cannot come where I go*, I adore Thee and I love Thee with all my heart.

O Jesus, the divine Word, who wast called a man possessed by the devil and a Samaritan, I adore Thee and I love Thee with all my heart.

O Jesus, model of sobriety, whom Thy enemies accused of loving wine and of feasting, I adore Thee and I love Thee with all my heart.

O Jesus, enemy of sin, but full of mercy towards the guilty, who wast called the friend of publicans and sinners, I adore Thee and I love Thee with all my heart.

O Jesus, the splendour of the Father and the image of His substance, who wast represented as a flagitious man, and a false prophet, I adore Thee and I love Thee with all my heart.

O Jesus, enemy of lies, who didst hear the Jews cast doubts upon the veracity of Thy words, when they ironically exclaimed: *Thou art not yet fifty years old, and Thou hast seen Abraham!* I adore Thee and I love Thee with all my heart.

O Jesus, God all powerful, who, in order to render Thyself conformable to our nature, with which Thou wast clothed, didst hide Thyself and leave the Temple, to avoid being stoned by Thy enemies, I adore Thee and I love Thee with all my heart.

O Jesus, only Son and faithful worshipper of the living God, who wast accused by the High Priest of having blasphemed and wast judged by him to be worthy of death, I adore Thee and I love Thee with all my heart.

O Jesus, King of Glory, who, full of meekness and of humility, didst allow Thy eyes to be blindfolded, Thy Face to be spit upon, and wounded by blows and buffets, I adore Thee and I love Thee with all my heart.

O Jesus, who dost search our hearts and our reins, and from whom nothing is hidden, who without complaint didst allow those insulting words to be addressed to Thee: *Prophesy unto us, O Christ, who is he that struck Thee?* I adore Thee and I love Thee with all my heart.

O Jesus, pacific King, accused of perverting the nation, of hindering the payment of tribute, of exciting the people to rebel, and of calling Thyself King and Messiah, I adore Thee and I love Thee with all my heart.

O Jesus, King of kings, despised by Herod and by his court, and clothed, in derision, with a white robe as a madman, I adore Thee and I love Thee with all my heart.

O Jesus, full of love, who didst hear the people cry out: *Put this man to death, and give up to us Barabbas. . . . May his blood fall on us and upon our children*, I adore Thee and I love Thee with all my heart.

O Jesus, King of heaven and earth, crowned with thorns, insolently struck and cruelly outraged by the words: *Hail King of the Jews*, I adore Thee and I love Thee with all my heart.

O Jesus, infinite goodness, the source of all creation, the sovereign master of the world, who didst listen to that sentence of death: *away with Him; away with Him; crucify Him; we have no king but Cæsar*, I adore Thee and I love Thee with all my heart.

O Jesus, worthy of all praise, who wast blasphemed on the Cross by the passersby, by the bad thief, by the chief priests, by the ancients of the people, by the cries and by the soldiers, I adore Thee and I love Thee with all my heart.

O Jesus, holy victim of sinners, who didst hear Thy enemies say: *He saved others, Himself He cannot save. Let Christ the king of Israel come down now from the cross, that we may see and believe,* I adore Thee and I love Thee with all my heart.

O Jesus, full of love, of confidence, and of reverence for Thy divine Father, who wast wounded with the most poignant anguish when the people cried out at the sight of Thee expiring: *He confided in God; let Him now deliver Him if He will have Him; for He said: I am the Son of God*, I adore Thee and I love Thee with all my heart.

# The Chaplet of the Holy Face[13]

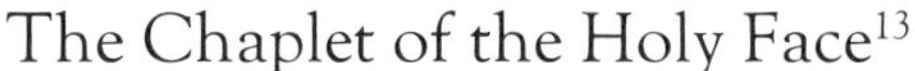


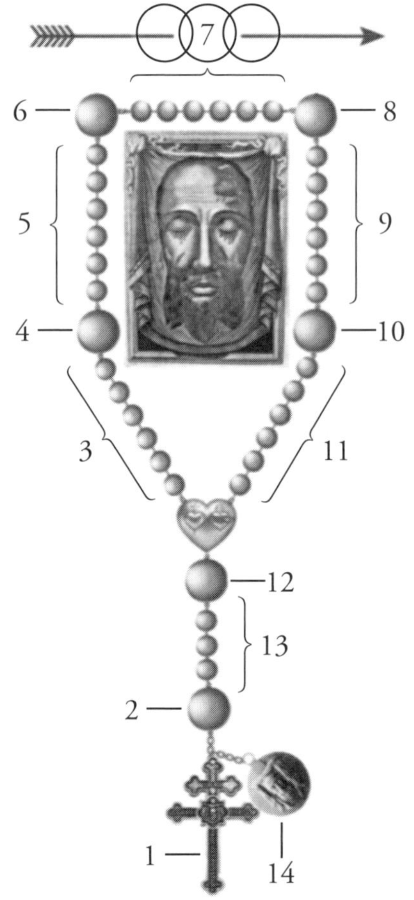


1. Make the Sign of the Cross. O God, come to my assistance; O Lord, make haste to help me. Glory be to the Father and to the Son and to the Holy Ghost. As it was in the beginning, is now, and ever shall be, world without end. Amen.

---

[13] To be prayed each day of the consecration.

2. My Jesus Mercy. In honor of the sense of **touch**. *Glory be...*

3. Arise, O Lord, and let Thy enemies be scattered, and let them that hate Thee flee from before Thy Face. (*Repeat 6 times*)

4. My Jesus Mercy. In honor of the sense of **hearing**. *Glory be...*

5. Arise, O Lord, and let Thy enemies be scattered, and let them that hate Thee flee from before Thy Face. (*Repeat 6 times*)

6. My Jesus Mercy. In honor of the sense of **sight**. *Glory be...*

7. Arise, O Lord, and let Thy enemies be scattered, and let them that hate Thee flee from before Thy Face. (*Repeat 6 times*)

8. My Jesus Mercy. In honor of the sense of **smell**. *Glory be...*

9. Arise, O Lord, and let Thy enemies be scattered, and let them that hate Thee flee from before Thy Face. (*Repeat 6 times*)

10. My Jesus Mercy. In honor of the sense of **taste**. *Glory be...*

11. Arise, O Lord, and let Thy enemies be scattered, and let them that hate Thee flee from before Thy Face. (*Repeat 6 times*)

12. My Jesus Mercy. Let us recall to mind the public life of the Savior and let us honor all the wounds of His adorable Face. *Glory be...*

13. Arise, O Lord, and let Thy enemies be scattered, and let them that hate Thee flee from before Thy Face. (*Repeat 3 times*)

14. (*On the Holy Face Medal*) God, our Protector, look on us, and cast Thine eyes upon the Face of Thy Christ. Amen.

15. (*On the crucifix*) Make the Sign of the Cross.

## *Additional Prayers*

Eternal Father, I offer Thee the Cross of Our Lord Jesus Christ and all the other instruments of His Holy Passion, that Thou may put division in the camp of Thine enemies, for as Thy beloved Son has said, "A kingdom divided against itself shall fall."

May the thrice Holy Name of God overthrow all their plans.

May the Name of the Living God split them up by disagreements.

May the terrible Name of the God of Eternity stamp out all their godlessness!

Lord, I do not desire the death of the sinner, but I want him to be converted and to live. Father, forgive them for they know not what they do.

# Day 1

## The Face of the Word of God

Let us adore the Holy Trinity! All happiness is contained within Himself. Each person, Father, Son, and Holy Ghost, gives to the others so perfectly and completely in love that each empties Himself for the others, making the Three-in-One Uncreated Being. He is so humble that He gives divine maternity to the Blessed Virgin Mary and even shares His divine nature with mere man![14] Perfect humility and perfect generosity exist in God. Since perfection remains in God, He has no need to create or to add to this perfection, because God is perfection, truth, goodness, and beauty itself. Creation does not add to His perfection, but it exemplifies His generosity. God is love, and He freely shares by creating out of nothing. His Word cannot be doubted, but it is creative.

God sees and contemplates Himself and sees not past or future but the eternal now. His greatness is that He exists without beginning or end. He gave mankind beginning, creating him out of nothing, as *imago Dei*![15] God's divinity is recognized in His Face, and mankind is made in this image. This Holy Face of the Word of God beholds "the brightness of his glory, and the figure of his substance."[16]

What an ineffable mystery that there exists a good God whose mysteries neither the angels nor mankind can penetrate. Let us contemplate this inaccessible light, the divine essence, as

---

[14] Those who follow the Ten Commandments and die in the state of grace will also share the divine nature.

[15] The image of God.

[16] Heb. 1:3.

the angels contemplate His Face with holy trembling and great generosity, veiling their faces with their wings, saying, *Sanctus, Sanctus, Sanctus, Dominus Deus Sabaoth.*[17] If you lack this desire, ask God to place this desire in your heart.

O my God, place upon my heart the desire to walk upon the road of suffering, that the virtues of humility and generosity may grow in my soul like wings of the eagle, spiraling upwards toward the Face of the Word of God on the ardent wind of the Holy Spirit. Place the Word in the very essence of my soul, so that I will have the determination to walk in this valley of tears which leads to union with Thee, now and in eternity. Amen.

## The Spiritual Age of Beginners

Theologians classify the three ages of the spiritual life as the purgative, illuminative, and unitive. The first eleven days of the Consecration to the Holy Face deal with the purgative way. The goal is to leave mortal sin forever.

Saint Teresa of Avila wrote that it takes *determined determination* to reject mortal sin and to freely progress through the spiritual life. In other words, the soul must be *generous* and never look back. "No man putting his hand to the plough, and looking back, is fit for the kingdom of God."[18] To be holy does not mean to be well-read, or a priest, or religious, but it means to be penetrated by the Gospel, to be aware of the Face of the Word of God looking into the very essence of one's soul.

Beginners have an "initial knowledge of themselves; little by little they discern the defects they have," moving in and out

---

[17] Holy, holy, holy, Lord God of armies!

[18] Luke 9:62.

of mortal sin or deliberate venial sin. They persevere until the dross of sin is removed by means of generosity and humility. But their humility is not mature as they see themselves in a superficial way and do not value the treasure of Baptism. They are unconscious of their egoism, which often reveals itself in a sharp reproach. They are taken by the world and have their minds filled with a thousand and one things,[19] making them unaware of the diamond embedded in the rough at his baptism. He is unaware of the great degree to which God loves him, sometimes thinking it best not to pray for himself. This is the height of pride! For the great command requires one to pray for oneself, "Love the Lord . . . and your neighbor as *yourself*."[20]

The beginner has a sensible love of God, reflecting on the parable: like the prodigal son or the woman caught in adultery. His love has not progressed to consider the various mysteries of salvation, like the four last things: death, judgment, heaven, and hell. Nor has he become like the eagle looking at the sun as he spirals upward and, on a fair sunny day, catches the rising heat pockets from the sun warming the earth.

The only beginners who will advance decide once and for all to root out mortal sin and voluntary sin. They must have a deep, voluntary love. "Love rendered everything savory to [Jesus]: labors and watchings, insults and mockeries, scourging and thorns, the Cross, and whatsoever things were prepared by the divine Will for the blissfulness of man."[21] The beginners who fail always want to take a shortcut. Instead of moving at

---

[19] Tanquerey, Very Rev. Adolphe, *The Spiritual Life*, no. 638, quoting St. Teresa of Avila, *Interior Castle*, 1st Mansion.

[20] Mark 12:30–31.

[21] Arnoudt, Rev. Peter J., S. J. *Imitation of the Sacred Heart of Jesus,* p. 270.

the speed of spiritual progress, as God has set, they run ahead of the Holy Ghost and fall flat on their faces. On the contrary, the true beginner is generous and abandons himself to Divine Providence, practicing the spiritual life in obedience, shunning excessive mortification,[22] and knowing the consolations of God will not last, because spiritual maturity desires only the God of all consolations, not just a spiritual happy place. But almost all beginners get complacent with spiritual consolations, falling into spiritual gluttony[23] and spiritual pride, comparing themselves as greater than others.

How does a beginner advance? He must endure the purification of the senses and accept suffering to the degree that God desires. When this happens, the beginner moves slowly from concerns of the flesh to those of the spirit. And God, who wishes us to progress more than the soul does, aids by placing the Passion of Jesus deepening the grove He traced at Baptism, showing the vanity of the world. Because it is "[t]hrough Baptism that we have been incorporated into Christ, and since we share His life we are to share His sentiments."[24] Then the soul begins a new life as when a child grows into an adolescent. The clue is this. During the crisis when God weans the soul of spiritual consolations, most souls are not generous enough and become stunted souls, whereas the generous souls are led by the

---

[22] Mortification is good, but if one does penance to oneself only to be noticed, it is secret pride. On the other hand, exterior penance and mortification driven by charity can help develop the habit of interior mortification with regard to the choice of sin (one thing that modern spiritual theology misses).

[23] Spiritual gluttony rather seeks the pleasures of the spirit instead of purity of soul and devotion to God.

[24] Tanquerey, Very Rev. Adolphe, *The Spiritual Life*, no. 737.

gift of the Holy Ghost of counsel. Thus, "He keeps us from all precipitation, from all levity, but above all, from all presumption so dangerous in spiritual ways."[25]

So, what level of generosity is required? At the soul's particular judgment,[26] how will the Face of the Word of God look upon her? Again, one must have a determined determination to please God no matter what the cost. Generosity must start at the very first moment, now. For when this becomes the known truth—that the way is narrow[27]—the intellect of the soul accepts or rejects the known truth. When one rejects what one knows as true, the intellectual power is damaged, and if repeated, the soul's thirst for truth is damaged forever. But the soul who accepts the known truth should eventually reach intimate union with the Face of God and, through hope, will see a benevolent Face at the particular judgment.

In conclusion, how does one arrive at the necessary level of generosity? Ask the Face of the Word in God to consider everyone greater than oneself because of one's hidden faults and another's hidden virtue.[28] This is humility; although not the most exalted virtue, it is the gateway through which the other virtues come.

Now, turn to the prayers to be recited during the *purgative* way and the Chaplet of the Holy Face (p. 15, 20).

---

25 Marmioin, Bl. Columba, *Christ the Life of the Soul*, p. 121.

26 Everyone has a particular judgment after his body and soul separate. This is where Jesus assigns him to heaven, purgatory, or hell. Then, at the general judgment, this sentence will be confirmed to the universe.

27 See Matt. 7:13–14.

28 *Summa Theologica* II–II, q. 161, a. 3.

# Day 2

## The Face of the Word and the Angels

Let us adore God, for in His infinite humility and wisdom, He creates the angels. Imagine the beauty of the choirs: pure spirits, closest in likeness to the divinity of God, made to adore Him with otherworldly chants. Saints who have heard a piece of the angelic symphony have gone into ecstasy for days.

Endowed with innumerable perfections, including free will, angels had a choice at the moment of their creation. A battle ensued.[29] In one instant, God tested the free will of the angels on various levels. He commanded adoration of the angels to Him. The less generous angels made a lukewarm submission. It was like a child who, being told to get ready for Mass, does it halfheartedly.

On the second level of testing, God told the angels that He would create beings endowed with both souls and bodies, who would be lesser than the pure angelic court, and that He would have His Son become incarnate in order for the species of the human race to be able to share in the divine nature. Again, the less generous angels failed the test, telling God that their nature, being higher than human, should receive the benefit of sharing in the divine nature. God also showed them the Face of Jesus at Nazareth, in the proclamation of the Kingdom of God, and during the Passion, Resurrection, and Ascension.

On the third level of testing, God revealed how, in the future, a woman named Mary, full of the grace of God, would be called the Mother of God, conceiving Jesus by the Holy Ghost and giving birth to Him who would save mankind. At

[29] Mary of Agreda, *Mystical City of God*, pp. 89–91.

this, they exclaimed, *Non serviam.* "I will not serve!" And they uttered their own downfall, being the first to blaspheme the Mother of God.

A pregnant silence filled heaven. After the blasphemies were vomited, the angels fell from their high places in an instant and were transformed into dragons and serpents, monsters of the most hideous complexion. After God's demotion of these revolutionists, the most generous of angels, Saint Michael[30] the Archangel, cried the first words of reparation, "*Quis est Deus*?" "Who is like unto God?" In God's divine wisdom and providence, He delegates Saint Michael and his companions to fight the revolutionists. God's providence is deep and difficult to understand. He appoints an angel from the second lowest rank of the nine choirs, a mere archangel, to have the honor of vanquishing the imposter, who, with the glance of the Holy Face of the Word shining on the serpents, was cast into hell to remain in reserve until the general judgment.[31]

Meanwhile, Saint Michael and the angels, who saw the Man-God in the veiled features of His human Face, piously prostrated their faces to the ground and raised the standard of reverence, reparation, and fidelity.

O my God, help me to see in every circumstance, pleasing or distasteful, Thy guiding hand of providence. May I be generous like Saint Michael and his companions when I see Thyself

---

[30] Saint Michael is one of the three special patrons of the Archconfraternity of the Holy Face. The other special patrons are Saint Martin of Tours and Saint Louis IX, king of France.

[31] Of course, some fallen angels are given freedom to roam the earth and tempt mankind. Part of the demons' punishment is to tempt souls. Generous souls reject the temptation and gain merit, and the demons continue to receive fresh punishments according to God's infinite justice.

visited with blasphemies by my impious generation. Help me to vehemently defend Thy thrice Holy Name and the dignity of the Most Blessed Ever Virgin Mary. Lastly, never let me be separated from Thee this day forward by mortal sin, and place in my very essence a desire for mortification so that I may live the Gospel without compromise.

## Mortification and Its Necessity

"Now I say to you: but unless you shall do penance, you shall all likewise perish."[32] The demons never advanced in the spiritual life from childhood and were defeated by the good angels. This battle, the growth or deformation of the spiritual life, currently progresses with our human family. What is the first step to take to advance from beginner to proficient in the spiritual life? Mortification.

Mortification means to kill all inordinate emotions, passions, or movements. These include inordinate movements of concupiscence,[33] anger, hatred, pride, hypocrisy, and so on.[34] The principal work of the purgative way is to kill inordinate movements and avoid falling back into sin. The soul does well to make an act of hope here, because God has brought one to read this far, knowing that the roots and consequences of these movements may continue to exist for a long time.

Remember, generosity is required in order to go forward. Otherwise, it is easy for souls to think that sin is only an offense or harm to men. But sin is a crime against the majesty of the

---

[32] Luke 13:3.

[33] The desire of the person's lower appetite, contrary to reason, which inclines him to sin against the sixth and ninth commandments.

[34] Garrigou-Lagrange, *The Three Ages of the Interior Life*, vol. 1, p. 282.

Godhead.[35] This is why Jesus had to remind Sr. Marie de St. Pierre of the gravity of breaking the first three commandments, which deal with God. Generosity is also required in an age that has lost its moral compass and considers the contemplative[36] life quite useless,[37] or only for the incompetent. God Himself wished to reply to this objection by canonizing a contemplative nun: Saint Thérèse of the Child Jesus and of the Holy Face, one of the pioneers to enroll in the Archconfraternity of the Holy Face in 1885! Generosity is required to realize the great means taken by Christ to save the world by the cross.

Saint Michael was quite generous in defending the rights of God. A mere archangel was called up as the angel to defend the Face of God. Generosity is required if the soul wishes to swim upstream, as this wicked generation declares that mortification does not belong to the essence of Christianity. This is a recipe for damnation.

According to the Gospel, mortification is death to sin, leading to a higher life. It results in great happiness in this life and the next. "Be you therefore perfect as also your heavenly Father is perfect."[38] Why? To see His Face! How? Christ brings us grace, which supernaturalizes us, making us higher than the angelic kingdom, directing us toward the possession of God through the Beatific Vision.[39]

---

[35] Tanquerey, Very Rev. Adolphe, *The Spiritual Life*, no. 715.

[36] To think about God and His creation, to talk to God and His court; an interior life of union with God.

[37] The heresy of *Americanism*, which sees little or no value in religious life of the monk or nun or those who spend time in adoration, was condemned by Pope Leo XIII.

[38] Matt. 5:48.

[39] Tanquerey, Very Rev. Adolphe, *The Spiritual Life*, no. 104.

God helps those who help themselves. The soul must battle the world, the flesh, and the devil by mortification through the means of the binding prayers.[40] The generous soul has the assistance of God, overcoming all resentment and animosity. Blessed are the meek. Christ preaches mortification of evil desire, evil gaze, and those who commit adultery in their hearts. Those who dress immodestly become accomplices to the mortal sin of those who sin in the heart, but Saint Paul says, "Let your modesty be known to all men."[41] How does one conquer these sins and temptations? The saints advise fasts, vigils, and other bodily austerities, which, when held in check, are a profitable servant whose strength must be preserved to place it at the soul's service.[42]

Mortification takes away egoism and engenders love of God and of neighbor. The mortified Christian is, as a rule, more truly happy than the worldling who abandons himself to every pleasure.[43] This patience and longanimity may break the anger of the adversary, and sometimes it converts him.[44]

---

40 Binding means to catch the devil and tie him up. Each person has sovereign authority to bind demons who tempt him in the name of Jesus. This is a necessary part of spiritual combat. For example, a short binding prayer may be: "In the Name of Jesus, I command you spirit of sloth to go to the foot of the cross."

41 Phil. 4:5.

42 Tanquerey, Very Rev. Adolphe, *The Spiritual Life*, no. 771.

43 Tanquerey, Very Rev. Adolphe, *The Spiritual Life*, no. 765.

44 There is a legend that the Good Thief, Saint Dismas, when he robbed the Holy Family, changed his course, perhaps seeing the Face of the Child Jesus. Later, when he saw the Face of Jesus on the cross, he asked Jesus to invite him into His Kingdom.

Mortification overcomes egoism. How many times do souls think they are right when they rashly judge? Mortification helps the soul become good by letting God, who knows everything in each heart, be the judge of others. The spiritual pride and hypocrisy make way for a humility where the soul sees all others as greater than himself, due to his hidden faults and their hidden virtue.

When fasting, the Lord calls for it to be done not in the sight of men. It should be done with charity and spiritual joy so it reaches the very root of evil by mortifying the craving for sensual pleasure.[45] "When we accomplish these acts of piety, it is not forbidden to be seen, but to *wish* to be seen, for we would lose the purity of intention, which ought to be directed immediately to the Father in the secret of our souls."[46]

Finally, a sign that a soul is on the road of mortification is gentleness. In order to be meek with those who revile us, souls must conquer themselves first. The next chapter looks at Adam and the Face of God. Since the fall of Adam, man lives in a fallen nature. But Christ, especially given in the Holy Eucharist, helps souls toward true mortification of sin and inordinate movements caused by our fallen nature. He does this by gentleness: Jesus was meek and humble of heart. If souls are mortified and persevere in the state of grace, which is first given at Baptism, they will see His most Holy Face.

Now, turn to the prayers to be recited during the *purgative* way and the Chaplet of the Holy Face (p. 15, 20).

---

[45] Tanquerey, Very Rev. Adolphe, *The Spiritual Life*, no. 749.

[46] Garrigou-Lagrange, pp. 283–84.

# Day 3

## The Face of God and Adam

I adore Thee, O Divine Majesty, who created us *ex nihilo*, "out of nothing." By saying Thy Word, Adam was created. Indeed, Thou has formed us above all other visible creatures. "And God saw all the things that he had made, and they were *very* good."[47] Help me to contemplate the fact that we are created in *imago Dei*,[48] "the image of God." How shall I understand how the countenance of Thy Holy Face is to be reflected in my face?

Did Adam and Eve see the Face of God? They "heard the voice of the Lord God walking in paradise at the afternoon air, Adam and his wife hid themselves from the face of the Lord God."[49] Adam and Eve possessed the preternatural gifts[50]—immortality, infused knowledge, and integrity—but were not able to see God Face to face. Once someone has the Beatific Vision, he cannot turn away from that vision: as Adam sinned, one must infer that he did not have that vision of God.[51] But those who die in the state of grace will have the Beatific Vision and never turn from His Face. How do we become partakers in this Beatific Vision, beholding the Face of God?

Remember humility? God fashions Adam[52] out of clay. He infuses an immortal soul into this human pottery, as if it were a spark of the divinity. "Remember man, thou art dust and unto

47 Gen. 1:31.

48 "Let us make man, said God, after our image and likeness" (Gen. 1:26).

49 Gen. 3:8.

50 No sickness or death, no need for experiential learning, no struggle with passions.

51 *Summa Theologica* I, q. 94, a. 1.

52 Adam means "earth."

dust thou will become."[53] When pride first begins to move in the soul, it needs to remember its origins: dirt![54] If souls check the movements of pride and the seven capital sins, they will be on their way to rooting out inordinate passions and begin to resemble God, who possesses spirit and heart.

Adam and Eve failed when they ate the fruit. They were cast out of the garden and could no longer eat from the Tree of Life, thus becoming mortals who were prone to death and losing the other preternatural gifts. But Divine Providence sent mankind a Redeemer who died on the new Tree of Life, whose fruit is His Body and Blood: "He that eateth my flesh and drinketh my blood, hath everlasting life: and I will raise him up in the last day."[55]

This new gift of eternal life, which is found in the Holy Mass at Holy Communion, impresses the image of God on the face of the communicant, expressing the spirit and heart of God. Much can be discerned by the face, and receiving the Body worthily[56] gives the face of faithful communicants a resemblance to the Face of God expressed in Jesus Christ, the New Adam.

"O God show us thy face, and we shall be saved."[57] We were born as children of wrath,[58] and Thou owed us nothing.

---

53 Ash Wednesday.

54 It is worth noting that the Vulgate gives the following translation: "The Lord God formed man out of the slime of the earth (*de limo terrae*) and breathed into his *face* the breath of life *and he became a living soul*" (Gen. 2:7). The first Adam had a face too.

55 John 6:55.

56 See 1 Cor. 11:29–30. Saint Paul speaks about how unworthy reception of Holy Communion leads to infirmity, weakness, and sleep.

57 Ps. 79:20.

58 See Eph. 2:3.

Withstanding Thy justice, Thou bestowed Thy gentle glance of mercy. Help us to see Thy tender loving mercy now, for it will only last a while, and then there is eternity. Help us to know our state as wayfarers and provide us the spark to do good and never abandon Thy way. Give us the grace to pray always, O Face of God; impress Thyself on my soul, transfigure it from light to light, that we may resemble Thee insofar as is possible.

## Sins to Be Avoided

In the previous chapters, souls wishing to advance in the spiritual life, into union with God, ultimately will be rewarded with heaven. Death is not the only requirement to be rewarded with heaven; rather, it is final perseverance in sanctifying grace. Soul, beg God for great generosity and for the desire to mortify, to put to death all sin. Equipped with generosity and mortification, the next step is to know what to kill—the sins to be avoided.

The capital sins of pride,[59] sloth, envy, anger, avarice, gluttony, and lust are less grave than heresy, apostasy, despair, and hatred of God.[60] They are capital because it is like the beginning or headway of a river; for example, the Arkansas River starts in

---

[59] See *Summa Theologica* II–II, q. 132, a. 4 where Saint Thomas quotes Saint Gregory (Moral. xxxi) where he numbers vainglory among the capital vices. Some recognize pride as one of the capital sins, not listing vainglory as a capital sin, and some recognize pride as the queen of all sins, thus allowing vainglory a place to be one of the capital sins. In the latter case, vainglory is considered an immediate offspring of pride, a disordinate desire for excellence.

[60] Garrigou-Lagrange, *The Three Ages of the Interior Life*, vol. 1, p. 299–300.

the Rocky Mountains, flows through Kansas, and grows into the Mississippi River. Instead of being cursed and driven out forever from the presence of God, as were the rebel angels, man was to have a Redeemer, thus, man, having a weaker intellect, falls by degrees.[61] The Mississippi river did not begin in a second, but by droplets of rain over months, flowing to the mighty river.

What is the root of the seven capital sins? It is inordinate self-love. This does not mean that we shouldn't love ourselves. But inordinate self-love is a defect—too much or too little. Some people separate themselves from the Face of God by never turning to Him. Many souls never pray for themselves. Inordinate self-love makes us turn our back on God, away from the source of happiness. We must mortify inordinate self-love so that an ordered self-love prevails.

The egotistical man loves himself more than God. The just man loves God above himself. The sinner's movement is downward, and the just man's movement is upward toward God.

"Inordinate self-love leads us to death, according to the Savior's words: 'He that loveth his life (in an egotistical manner) shall lose it; and he that hateth (or sacrifices) his life in this world keepeth it unto life eternal.'"[62] The key to overcoming self-love is to acknowledge that we are contemptible due to our inordinate self-love.

The world, the flesh, and the devil are the three sources of inordinate self-love. Sins of the flesh, although more shameful, are not as depraved as sins of pride, for the latter are more directly opposed to God.[63]

---

[61] Marmiaon, Bl. Columba, *Christ in His Mysteries*, p. 97.

[62] Garrigou-Lagrange, p. 300, quoting John 12:25.

[63] *Summa Theologica* I–II, q. 77, a. 5.

Pride is considered more than a capital sin because four capital sins proceed from it:

1. Vanity, inordinate love of praise and honors, engenders disobedience, boasting, hypocrisy, contention through rivalry, discord, love of novelties, and stubbornness.
2. Spiritual sloth, sadness of the soul at the thought of labor in sanctification, engenders malice, rancor, or bitterness toward neighbor, pusillanimity in the face of duty, discouragement, spiritual torpor, forgetfulness of the precepts, and seeking after forbidden things.
3. Envy inclines us to grow sad over another's good and engenders hatred, slander, calumny, and joy at the misfortune of another.
4. Anger, when it is not just indignation but a sin, is an inordinate movement of the soul which inclines us to repulse violently what displeases us. It engenders quarrels, insults, and abusive words.

Overall, these vices weigh down a soul and keep it from spiritual peace and joy. The opposing virtues engender a peace that the world cannot give, a constant conversation with God, and living heaven now as a seed of what is to come. But first, these vices must be dealt with in these first eleven days before the soul may know virtue, as seen in the illuminative way (days 12–22) and lived in the unitive way (days 23–33).

The next step is to make the examination of conscience. This means looking at all the times we had inordinate self-love.

Clergy and religious do this every night at Compline.[64] The spiritual masters recommend examining the conscience several times a day. This means looking at our failures and asking God to see ourselves as He sees us, not in a scrupulous[65] way, but by asking for the gift of wisdom to see ourselves as God sees us. Over time, considering one's faults inside God's mercy helps one to gaze at God and not self. God only wants us to try not to sin. Once we begin living with generosity, mortification, and knowledge of what sin is, we are moving in the right direction, and our confidence in God will only increase.

Before concluding, it is important to touch on sins of ignorance, frailty, and malice.

Invincible ignorance excuses one from sin because he has done everything he could to know what is right and wrong before the moral act. But vincible ignorance is a sin when one purposefully chooses not to be informed of sin and then commits sin based on that ignorance.

Sins of frailty deal with strong passions which impel the will to give into sin. Sometimes these can still be mortal sins. One example is the first pope, Saint Peter, who denied Jesus three times. His intense passion and fear impelled him to deny Christ. "And the Lord turning looked on Peter. And Peter remembered the word of the Lord, as he had said: Before the cock crow, thou shalt deny me thrice. And Peter going out, wept bitterly."[66] With sins of frailty, a soul can resist, and should resist in the beginning. Don't let the devil have that crack in

---

[64] Compline ("Completion") Psalms are said at the close of the day from the Divine Office.

[65] Scrupulosity means one who erroneously believes he is guilty of mortal sin, and that he is therefore seldom in the state of grace.

[66] Luke 22:61–62.

the door to the soul given to him, because then he becomes a strong man[67] and slams the door, making one fall.

The sin of malice means choosing evil knowingly. These were the sins of the devil; with calculated deliberation, the fallen angels made their choice and will never repent of it. The demons saw all the good and the bad by virtue of their superior intellect, so they committed the grave sin of malice.[68] For example, rejecting the known truth is so malevolent that the sinner rejects the very thing that would save him or deliver him from evil.

So, sin is the much more grave as it is voluntary. But good is more powerful than evil, and each soul has the means to overcome any sin now and wherever he finds the state of the soul. The love of Christ dying on the cross pleased God more than all the sins taken together displeased Him.

Now, turn to the prayers to be recited during the *purgative* way and the Chaplet of the Holy Face (p. 15, 20).

## Day 4

### The Face of God and the Patriarchs

Let us adore God, saying by the mouth of the Holy Ghost, "Fear of the Lord is the beginning of wisdom."[69] Yes, it truly is wise to fear God, not as a servile fear, but to fear Him because of His infinite power, goodness, and beauty. The patriarchs had this fear and made it fertile ground for their souls and the souls of their progeny. Today, the enemies of God propagate their war

[67] See Matt. 12:24.

[68] Agreda, Ven. Mary, *Mystical City of God*, Vol. 1, p, 86.

[69] Prov. 9:10.

machine of fear and anxiety by false narratives that cause such anxiety in people that it compromises their minds and immune systems, causing one of the greatest mortality crises in history.

The Face of God spoke to the patriarchs, giving them a good fear of God, the kind that augments blessings. God "conversed with Abraham as a friend with a friend."[70] Some say that the father of the Hebrew nation saw the Holy Trinity come in the form of three angels, and Abraham prostrated his face to the ground. This was a rare encounter because most patriarchs only heard the voice of God.

But Moses, full of generosity,[71] had the privilege to speak with God frequently. Moses asked Him if he could see His Face. Moses said: "Shew me thy glory." God replied: "Thou canst not see my face: for man shall not see me and live. And again he said: Behold there is a place with me, and thou shalt stand upon the rock. And when my glory shall pass, I will set thee in a hole of the rock, and protect thee with my right hand, till I pass: And I will take away my hand, and thou shalt see my back parts: but my face thou canst not see."[72]

Saint Teresa remarks: "The devil strives to make us think it pride to entertain lofty desires, and to wish to imitate the saints; but it is of a great service to encourage ourselves with the desire of great things, because, although the soul has not all at once the necessary strength, yet she nevertheless makes a bold fight, and rapidly advances."[73]

---

[70] Fourault, *The Month of the Holy Face*, p. 48.

[71] Note how important a generous soul is required for the blessings of God!

[72] Ex. 33:18, 20–23.

[73] Teresa of Avila, *Life*, ch. 13 from St. Alphonsus Liguori, *The Holy Eucharist*, p. 336.

This is why Moses came down the mountain shrouded with such radiance that the people asked him to wear a veil over his face so as not to blind them when preaching. He is depicted in pictures with two horns of light emanating from his brow to indicate this wonderful spectacle, because he was gifted to see the Face of God through the cloud.

Yet, the Eucharistic Face of God is seen through a thinner cloud or veil and dwells within souls generous enough to receive Him in their bosom in the state of grace.[74] "He that eateth my flesh, and drinketh my blood, hath everlasting life: and I will raise him up in the last day. For my flesh is meat indeed: and my blood is drink indeed. He that eateth my flesh, and drinketh my blood, abideth in me, and I in him."[75]

O dear Holy Face of the patriarchs, help us to live as to one day see Thee Face to face. Never let me be separated from Thee as I beg of Thee to reveal to me my predominant fault so that I may see Thee as did Abraham, Moses, and Mary. Our Lady of the Holy Name of God, intercede for me so that any fear that comes from the world will turn into the fear that leads to wisdom in God. Press the Face of your child Jesus to your bosom for me and look at His Face with love for me.

## The Predominant Fault

What is the predominant fault? It is our main defect. Some temperaments are inclined to effeminacy, indolence, sloth, gluttony, and sensuality. Others are inclined to pride and anger.

---

[74] See 1 Cor. 11:29–30.

[75] John 6:55–57.

It is our domestic enemy, and if it grows, it may ruin our destiny to grow in the interior life.

How do we recognize the predominant fault? Our enemy, the devil, knows it, for it is the weakest part of our soul. His tactic is to throw everything he has at our weakest links or vices to break down the armor of the theological and moral virtues.[76]

But how can we find this predominant fault? Again, we must ask God for generosity and docility. There are many ways to discover it. If you are really generous and courageous, ask those who live with you. It would help to ask a director or confessor. "Father, do you know what my predominant fault is? Can you help me to discover it?" Also, tendencies are revealed in silence and solitude, whether in prayer or work. Through frequent and fervent prayer, ask God for light: the eyes of the mind shall be opened, so as to see clearly that the wisdom of the world—which abhors the love of wholesome humiliations and mortifications is true folly; but that the salutary love coming down from Heaven, taught by word and example, is purest wisdom.[77]

Review the virtues and opposing vices of the spiritual patrimony of the Church.[78] Then ask yourself, "What is generally the cause of my sadness or joy?" For sadness, it could be rash judgments, going over past hurts, or anxiety for the future. For joy, it may include Mass, being industrious, saying the Rosary, or making consistent meditation.

---

76 The theological virtues are faith, hope, and love. The moral virtues are prudence, justice, temperance, and fortitude.

77 Arnoudt, Rev. Peter J., S. J. *Imitation of the Sacred Heart of Jesus,* p. 272.

78 To name just two of many sources, *Summa Theologica* I–II of St. Thomas Aquinas and the monastic writings of John Cassian, *The Institutes or the Conferences.*

If the predominant fault has reigned in us, it hates being unmasked and will find any excuse to remain hidden. The discernment of spirits is a good thing to ask of God.

It is also helpful to recognize, by paying attention to which temptations visit us. If the soul binds these in the name of Jesus, sending them to the foot of the cross, this is a breakthrough in the way of the interior life. When moments of fervor from the Holy Ghost arrive, ask Him to reveal the fault and offer it to Him to burn it with His ardent love.

Jesus called Saint John one of the sons of thunder because he wanted to call down fire from heaven on his enemies. But Jesus, taking the apostles aside and gently teaching them His Way, changed Saint John into a gentle lion. At the end of his life, he was old and crippled, and was carried on a mat around his flock, encouraging the crowds, "Love one another! Love one another!"

How does one combat the predominant fault? "Because the predominant fault is our principal interior enemy, we must combat it. When it is conquered, temptations are no longer very dangerous, but are rather occasions of progress."[79]

Beg for generosity and to have a deep piety and stable interior life. Otherwise, there will be no rooting out the predominant fault, and thus no real growth. Before this fault is removed, virtues are more, so to speak, inclinations, not virtues. This is because mortal sin is still a part of life, and no merit is rewarded in a state of wrath in relation to God.

The three-pronged approach to victory is prayer, examination of conscience, and penance. Prayer must be sincere.

---

[79] Garrigou-Lagrange, *The Three Ages of the Interior Life*, vol. 1, p. 318.

Keep track weekly how many times you have fallen into the predominant fault. The financially astute use the instrument of a budget and track their spending. Just like the thrifty, this method is also important to become spiritually astute.

The penance helps sanctify the soul. For men, when taking a double look at a woman, the second look being out of curiosity or lust, say a prayer for purity and custody of the eyes. For women, when tempted to dress immodestly, ask for the grace that your modesty may be known to the world. Venerable Leo DuPont would punch people near the ear when they blasphemed or were immodestly clothed. He became gentler later in life, progressing in the spiritual life, first giving twenty-five cents for each block the streetcar driver would omit blasphemy, until finally, when the holy man heard blasphemy, he asked those who uttered those vain words to punch him!

Do not let the smallness of soul, which is called pusillanimity, derail progress. This leads the soul to think the predominant fault cannot be eradicated, but we must never make peace with our faults. This battle is for each of us, not just for the saint. But the royal road of suffering is the only way to joy and peace because it comes from a spirit of sacrifice.

How does one know the predominant fault is eradicated? Love of God and love of souls gains the highroad. That is why Jesus created the Church: for right worship of God and salvation of souls. Once the souls overcome the predominant fault, God uses them to help extend the Kingdom of God. This is when life gets exciting. Saints are attractive. And souls will want to surround you because your life is becoming beautiful. You are moving from the egomaniac, who has a constant conniving conversation with self, and beginning to move toward a constant conversation with God. At this point, heaven will begin to well within you. But there are still seven more steps before illumination begins in the souls. Next, we see the Face of Jesus in the stable and the passions to be regulated.

Now, turn to the prayers to be recited during the *purgative* way and the Chaplet of the Holy Face (p. 15, 20).

## Day 5

### The Face of Jesus in the Manger

Like a flash of lightning which illuminates the skies or the sunbeam which dissipates the clouds, the Face of Jesus pierces the darkness of the world of fallen mankind as He rests on the ground moments after birth. The Redeemer of humanity visits us amidst the poverty of a stable, reminding us of the profound humility of our God.

As Mary and Joseph had traveled from Nazareth to Bethlehem to fulfill the dictates of the government, they were suffering fatigue and hunger. Finding no opening at the inns, Joseph remembered the barn of animals nearby the city proper, and Baby Jesus was born there.

The angels sing, "Glory to God in the highest."[80] Mary and Joseph contemplate the Babe's smiling Face; meanwhile, two animals give the child warmth on the cold night. There is no greater love on earth than the love of Mary, Joseph, and the angels toward Jesus. This kind of charity is the perfect union, as the Redeemer says later, "Be you therefore perfect as also your heavenly Father is perfect."[81] The contemplation of God

[80] Luke 2:14.

[81] Matt. 5:48.

by Mary and Joseph has profoundly changed with the advent of the Infant God who comes as the restorer of a fallen world to give man a perfect model of virtues and to give Himself as pure love, for He is no longer just the promise of the prophets, but He is the Word made flesh.

Mary and Joseph are the representatives of humanity, and each day, their union with God grows deeper and deeper—so should our interior life.

The passions of human frailty must be removed in order to arrive at greater union. Purging the senses must be accomplished before the purging of the imagination and the intellect.

O Lord, let a ray of Thy Holy Face illuminate my soul and purge it of all disordered senses; let the smile of Thy lips strengthen me to higher degrees of generosity; let the glance from Thy divine eyes burn in my heart a divine flame that will never be extinguished. O Mary and Joseph, intercede for me so that I may purge all the dross that prevents me from the union that my Infant God desires of me.

## Regulating the Passions and Purification of the Senses

At this point, the soul is almost halfway through the purgative way and equipped with a greater understanding of the need for generosity, mortification, avoidance of sin, and it now desires to know and root out the predominant fault. This is when most souls waver and fail. In order to advance, one must make an act of faith. Yes, hell is real for the soul which dies without repenting of mortal sin. The path to heaven has been made crystal clear through Christ, who is the Fullness of Divine Revelation, and God's grace makes it possible to obtain.

The preceding four days presented to the mind generosity, mortification, capital sins, and the predominant fault. It is one thing to learn about these principles, but it may take a lifetime to put them into practice. The consequences of original sin, the effects of personal sin, the reward of the Beatific Vision, and the necessity of carrying the cross require mortification to render the soul open to the grace in order to advance into union with God.

Saint John of the Cross expounds the faults of beginners: "It is vanity and delusion to glory in beauty, gracefulness, physical constitution, or in particular mental endowments."[82] What is necessary?

1. Follow the Commandments; beg God to help one see himself as God sees the soul. This is wisdom which is a mature fear of God. Beg Him to know hidden offenses against the precepts, especially the supreme precept of love of God and neighbor.
2. Guard yourself better against deliberate venial sin.
3. Suppress imperfections, which is choosing a lesser good over a greater good or a lesser act of generosity.
4. Beg God fervently for a greater light to see the gravity of sin and to have a greater contrition for sin.
5. Lastly, avoid repeated venial sin because easily committing venial sins loses purity of intention, eventually leading one to mortal sin.

---

[82] St. John of the Cross, *Ascent of Mount Carmel*, Bk. III, Ch. XX.

## The Mortification of the Flesh

The only way to overcome most sins is to fight or fly from them. But the only way to overcome lust is by flight.[83] Direct resistance to lust does not work. Instead of looking for these, we must flee from them as we would a dangerous reptile.[84] However, spiritual sloth is overcome by resistance.

Avoid even indirect voluntary movements of the flesh with binding prayers.[85] Chastity and continence are not only not harmful, but even commendable from a purely medical point of view, but also allow one to enjoy Our Lord's company.[86] True love of God is centered on the will rather than on feelings or spiritual gluttony. Saint John of the Cross says, "Many beginners, delighting in the sweetness and joy of their spiritual occupations, strive after spiritual sweetness rather than after pure and true devotion."[87]

Know the two types of mysticism. "By their fruits you shall know them."[88] There is nothing higher on earth than true mysticism. The saints had it, and the saints were attractive. True mys-

---

83 *Summa Theologica* II–II, q. 35, a. 1, ad. 4um.

84 Tanquerey, Very Rev. Adolphe, *The Spiritual Life*, no. 878.

85 In the name of Jesus Christ, the intercession of the Blessed Virgin Mary, my patron saint N., I command you spirits of lust to go and adore the Holy Trinity, Father, Son, and Holy Ghost, to receive an attack from your nemesis or nemeses, the instruments of the Passion, and to suffer the most excruciating pain for the next fifteen minutes. (This is one example of a binding prayer.) See *ST* II–II, q. 90, a. 2 A layperson may lawfully use the name of God to adjure the demons for himself but not for others.

86 Tanquerey, Very Rev. Adolphe, *The Spiritual Life*, no. 877.

87 John of the Cross, *The Dark Night*, Bk. I, Ch. 6.

88 Matt. 7:16.

ticism is the key to heaven and the treasure of God's charity and gifts of the Holy Ghost. The worst is a false mysticism, which is a false love of God and neighbor. It is like the difference between gold and imitation gold.

## Mortification of Anger[89]

What is the greatest test that shows a soul prays well? "Love your enemies: do good to them that hate you: and *pray* for them that persecute and calumniate you."[90] Pray for one's enemies. One of the greatest roadblocks to advance in the interior life is dwelling on past hurts, real or perceived. Offer these to God through the Immaculate Heart of Mary. Ask the Holy Face, as the Infant God, to shine His rays on your soul in the darkness of temptations to anger.

The Christian who does not sharply defend his rights but thinks more of duties often wins over his irritated brother, whom he calms by patience and meekness.[91] Looking at the Holy Face draws one to intuit that Its wounds speak of love: "But if one strike thee on the right cheek, turn to him also the other."[92] Is this not the most sure way to arrive at the inner life of God and a likeness to Him in heaven?

But meekness is not to be confused with effeminacy. Effeminacy is the tendency to let everything go because of a lack of energy or just being afraid to act. Inordinate anger usually means a soul is wounded. A meek person does not judge or

---

89 Or irascible appetite.

90 Matt. 5:44.

91 Garrigou-Lagrange, *The Three Ages of the Interior Life*, vol. 1, p. 339.

92 Matt. 5:39.

speak evil of anyone because he believes that everyone is better than he is.[93]

Mortification is most necessary as anger is serious, "because the impious utter evil words and blaspheme the holy Name of God, spit in the face of the Saviour and cover it with mud."[94] Blasphemy is one of the two offenses to which devotees of the Holy Face make reparation. Meekness mitigates the passion of anger[95] making way for charity to flower and its fruits to mature.

Some souls wish to outrun the Holy Ghost. They think they can become saints in one day. Saint John of the Cross calls it "bitter zeal." The more they fall, the angrier they become. The only remedy for this is the dark night, where spiritual meekness is made active in the soul.

If done well, the soul choosing active purification of the flesh and anger is well on its way to gaining spiritual momentum. These active purifications produce a certain simplicity of soul comparable to that of the shepherds and the magi. Sin is complicated, and when it is purged, the soul is simple, or lighter, so to speak. The next chapter deals with purification of the imagination, memory, intellect, and will.

Now, turn to the prayers to be recited during the *purgative* way and the Chaplet of the Holy Face (p. 15, 20).

---

93 Bergamo, Padre Gaetano, *Humility of Heart*, p. 172.

94 Janvier, Abbé, *Manual of the Archconfraternity of the Holy Face*, p. 103.

95 *ST* II–II, q. 57, a. 4.

# Day 6

## The Shepherds and the Magi before the Holy Face

O most powerful God, Thou who hast infinite power in Thy divine simplicity while at the same time holds perfect humility. Divine Face of the Infant God who, in thirty years from birth held a child in Thy arms and didst say, "Amen I say to you, unless you be converted, and become as little children, you shall not enter into the kingdom of heaven."[96] Show Thy Face to those who, in contemplating Thy goodness, may become like Thee, the child in the crib and the child held in Thy arms.

What encouragement to see the shepherds hastening to see Thy Countenance. After Saint Joseph and Mary ever Virgin, these are the first of mankind to gaze on Thy Face.

Lowest and poorest of His creatures, they adore the Child suffering with Him who appears beneath the veil of poverty. But what do they see? The invisible ray of grace penetrates their simple, childlike souls, making an abundant fountain of respect, love, and praise flow forth.

But the Child is not for them alone. Behold the Magi, rich with power, wealth, and wisdom, who represent the Gentiles. Despite their wealth, their attachment is not of this world but of another world. In their wisdom, and with the eyes of their souls always gazing upward, the magi recognized the star: "Nothing was capable of stopping them until they found the real star of Jacob."[97] What of their encounter? They prostrate

[96] Matt. 18:3.

[97] Fourault, *The Month of the Holy Face*, p. 68.

themselves and adore the Face of Jesus, brighter than the sun, "more lovely than the moon, fresher than the roses of spring."[98]

They share their wealth with Jesus. The gold of charity is given as a symbol of the purification of the will. The incense of prayer is given as a symbol never to forget the presence of God. And the myrrh of mortification is given as a symbol to kill sin. What does the Holy Face do? He gives a look of encouragement in exchange. Dear reader, what a joy it will be to see the same Face of encouragement at our particular judgment. How does one make that happen? Keep moving through the stages of the purgative way by active purification of the imagination, memory, and intellect. Thus, the magi "departed for the country by another way," as if to say they encountered the Holy Face of Jesus and, in a spiritual sense, went "another way." After encountering the Holy Face, they were changed forever and were now following "another way."

## Active Purification of the Imagination, Memory, and Intellect

"Mary must shine forth more than ever in mercy in the might and in grace in these latter times."[99] In an age of graphic pornography, the Blessed Virgin Mary is a great means to purify bad images in the memory. Turn to her, and God will show mercy through her might and grace. After making the Total Consecration to Mary, she aids the soul to make the Total Consecration to the Holy Face of Jesus. What steps are necessary to advance in this mystical combat?

---

[98] Litany of the Holy Face, Sr. Marie de St. Pierre.

[99] Louis de Montfort, *True Devotion to Mary*, p. 29.

Active purification of the imagination is required so the soul will consider divine things and not vain, inconsistent, fantastic, or even forbidden things. In the beginning, it is hard to dispel dangerous images, but over time, and with the help of grace, it will become easier to contemplate God instead. Removing worldly images through discipline of the imagination will enable the soul to meditate on passages in the Gospel, like the shepherds seeing the Face of the Infant God or Peter seeing the Face of Christ and weeping after his triple denial. The mind will then be able to reflect on the superior idea which these mysteries express, like the need for reparation.

How does one purify the imagination? Spirituality 101 will help. Stop looking at bad images. Stop thinking of bad images. Making these acts of renunciation over time, the will and intellect will gradually dominate the imagination. This produces an "obedient" imagination which will thirst after divine liturgies like a Solemn High Mass, Rorate[100] Mass, or a Pontifical High Mass.[101]

Why does the memory need to be purified? Due to original sin, repeated sins of the past have recorded useless and dangerous memories. For example, our minds are usually dominated by past hurts from our neighbor instead of his favors toward us. But the chief defect of memory is forgetfulness of God. Forgetfulness of God immerses the soul in time rather than eternity. Egalitarianism, seeing everything from a horizontal, this-worldly perspective, prevents us from gaining wisdom,

---

[100] *Rorate*: A Mass only with candlelight during an early morning on a Saturday of Advent.

[101] *Pontifical High Mass*: A sung Mass celebrated by a bishop, deacon, sub-deacon and assistant priest.

which sees things as God sees them: from the standpoint of hierarchy. He sees time from the top of a mountain, looking down at all the ages at a glance. Remembering God helps the soul recognize the value of time as a means to God.

But how does one remember God? He must be healed by hope of eternal beatitude.[102] Devotion to the Holy Face of Jesus is one of the last devotions[103] given to mankind because it deals with the Beatific Vision, the end for which we exist. Devotion to the Holy Face helps us remember God, especially His first three commandments against the sins of idolatry, blasphemy, and irreverence. "In all thy works remember the last end, and thou shalt never sin."[104]

Purification of the memory requires forgetfulness of all creatures in order to find the Creator,[105] meditation on death,[106] avoiding anxiety about one's affairs,[107] and avoiding vain and worldly learning.[108] In some sacristies hangs the epitaph, "Remember priest, celebrate this Mass as if it were your first Mass, your only Mass, and your last Mass." It reminds the priest to be reflective of the divine at Mass. Lastly, a soul must order

---

[102] John of the Cross, *The Ascent of Mount Carmel*, Bk. III, ch. 6 f. Hope, he says, is so much the greater as the memory is empty of notions of created things.

[103] In particular, the modern form was given to Sr. Marie de St. Pierre in the 1840s. But devotion to the Holy Face in general is ancient and started with Adam.

[104] Ecclus. 7:40.

[105] Thomas à Kempis, *The Imitation of Christ*, Bk. III, ch. 31.

[106] Thomas à Kempis, Bk. I, ch. 23.

[107] Thomas à Kempis, Bk. III, ch. 39.

[108] Thomas à Kempis, Bk. III, ch. 43.

himself in every deed and thought as if he were immediately to die in order to purify the memory.

Why does the intellect need to be purified? It needs to be purified due to original sin and our personal sins. Baptism does this, but the innocence from Baptism is often lost through our personal sins. Man's intellect is wounded and ignorant, and instead of tending to the supreme Truth, it gets stuck on earthly things. But God reveals Himself to us to encourage us to know supreme Truth. A soul may know truth apart from revelation, but it will take a considerable amount of time. Although Baptism gives sanctifying grace, this wound can get reopened, especially by curiosity and spiritual pride. Curiosity goes after less useful subjects instead of God and our salvation. It is like collecting too many things. Poverty helps one to be free from clutter. To combat vain curiosity, we must call to mind that whatever is not eternal is not worthy of winning and captivating the thought of immortal beings such as we are.[109] Spiritual pride is worse because one relies on his own judgment and not the counsel of others. Unchecked, this can lead to spiritual blindness, like that of the Pharisees. In these souls, God withdraws His light. The dullness of mind leads these souls to grave folly—for example, communism or socialism, a "doctrine of class war as the universal agent of social progress."[110] The conflict between Christ as King and false universalism must be met with the prayers in the Holy Face Devotion by souls consecrated to His Face.

How does one directly remedy the disorder of spiritual pride and blindness? Faith. Faith requires two things: first,

---

[109] Tanquerey, Very Rev. Adolphe, *The Spiritual Life*, no. 201.

[110] Sheed, Frank, *Commiunism and Man*, p. 47.

adhering to all revealed truths, and second, judging all things according to those truths.

Saint John of the Cross says that acts of adhering to revealed mysteries that are obscure actually enlighten us in that mystery and strengthens our adherence to it. In other words, acts of faith strengthen our faith.[111] The obscurity of faith is preparation for the Beatific Vision. Consecration to the Holy Face of Jesus and living the devotion according to the six[112] conditions drives souls toward the Beatific Vision. "To see the intimate life of God, a person would have to die and receive the Beatific Vision. Now faith makes us attain here on earth this inner life of God in obscurity."[113]

To sum up, active purification means to overcome curiosity by no longer preferring vain study of secondary matters, but instead to probe into the "one thing . . . necessary."[114] It means that in order to overcome spiritual pride, we must avoid rash judgment and tenacity in our own judgment and, rather, practice docility. While learned men discourse endlessly without being able to reach a conclusion, God gave us the shepherds at the stable, who with a clean heart intuited the obscure mystery

---

[111] John of the Cross, *The Ascent of Mount Carmel*, Bk. II, ch. 11; Faith is a dark night for the soul.

[112] In the *Manual of the Archconfraternity of the Holy Face*, elevated to that rank by Pope Leo XIII in 1885, the six conditions for members include 1. To be inscribed on the roll; 2. Receive the rule and certificate of admission; 3. Everyday recite *O Lord show us thy Face and we shall be saved*, a *Pater, Ave,* and *Gloria Patri*; 4. Wear an effigy of the Holy Face; 5. Assist as far as possible the monthly meetings; and 6. Propagate to the utmost of our power the devotion to the suffering Face of our Lord.

[113] Garrigou-Lagrange, *The Three Ages of the Interior Life*, vol. 1, p. 361.

[114] Luke 10:42.

of the Incarnation and became the first contemplatives of the Holy Face of God incarnate.

Now, turn to the prayers to be recited during the *purgative* way and the Chaplet of the Holy Face (p. 15, 20).

# Day 7

## The Face of Jesus in the Temple

Let us adore the Face of Jesus as we travel from Bethlehem to the Temple. Recall the great poverty of the Holy Family: no room at an inn, the Face warmed by an ox and a donkey. Enter the precincts of the house of God as Jesus is to be presented to His Father as King of heaven and earth.

Two doves are offered as ransom for the Blessed Virgin's purification. Simeon has been waiting for the Messiah, as he was told that he would see Him before his death. Anna, living as a prototype for members of the Confraternities of the Holy Face, "departed not from the temple by fasting and prayers serving God night and day."[115]

Imagine the secret ray of grace warming the hearts of these two outstanding pillars of reparation and reverence. Simeon, with his eyes bathed in tears, pressed Jesus against his aged breast and broke into prophecy the words many clerics say at Compline![116] "Because my eyes have seen thy salvation, which thou hast prepared before the *face* of all the peoples."[117]

---

[115] Luke 2:37.

[116] Compline: night Psalms from the Divine Office. The Roman Ritual requires nightly the *Nunc dimittis.*

[117] Luke 2:30–31.

After Simeon places the child back in the arms of His mother, he continues to prophesy: "This child is set for the fall, and the resurrection of many in Israel, and for a sign which shall be contradicted. And thy own soul a sword shall pierce."[118]

The fall includes the mighty of the world who will be humbled at the general judgment. The resurrection includes the humble who will be exalted in the valley of Josaphat, given the power of judging on thrones.

God tries those whom He loves. God has a great reward for those who meritoriously suffer much. The cup of suffering is a sign of those who accept the royal road of suffering and advance in the way of purification of the will.

The Holy Face Chaplet honors the Seven Dolors of the Blessed Virgin Mary by praying seven *Gloria Patris* in her honor. Her soul was transpierced with grief, but it now delights in paradise. May our souls follow where our Mother leads!

My God, help me to meditate on the Holy Face at the Temple. Help me to participate in the hidden graces today just as Simeon and Anna did at the Temple. Make me to know the obstacles of grace working in my soul. Show these obstacles at the moment I am about to face them. Give me the strength to remove them, and if I do not, take them from me even though I should suffer greatly. Grant that my life here may be like eternal life begun: to see Thy Face.

## Purification of the Will

A man is either good or bad. He either wills good as a whole or he is an egoist. The will is defined as the power that tends

---

[118] Luke 2:34–35.

toward the good known through the intellect. When a man wills a lesser good than he ought, this is said to be a defect. The principal defect of the will is self-love. Because of original sin, we are born without charity, our wills are turned away from God, "and [we] were by nature children of wrath."[119] The wound of inordinate self-love is called the wound of malice. Baptism restores us from wrath to adopted sons, but this wound remains after Baptism and is in the process of healing and often is reopened by personal sin. Since the principal defect is inordinate self-love or lack of rectitude, the soul forgets the love due to God. But the strength of the virtuous will is abandonment to Divine Providence or *docility* to God.

So how does one purify the will? It is by progress in the love of God. One must submit himself totally to God by docility to Providence, practicing the moral virtues: justice, rendering each his due; religion, rendering God His due; reparation, repairing injury due to sin; but above all, charity, our love of God and neighbor.

Charity reminds the soul to serve God and neighbor above self. One must have an ordinate love of self with the spirit of sacrifice. "Holiness for us must be based before and above all upon the fulfillment of the divine law and the natural law, the precepts of the decalogue, the commandments of the Church, and the duties of our state."[120]

What is the best way to pray to purify the will? Saint Paul fell to the ground after Jesus spoke to him and asked, "Lord, what wilt thou have me to do?"[121]

---

[119] Eph. 2:3.

[120] Marmion, Bl. Columbo, *Christ in His Mysteries*, p. 227.

[121] Acts 9:6.

Like Saint Paul, with repeated faults against Christ, purification of the will is difficult, but with the aid of divine grace, the love of God can grow in us.

Progress is not always constant, but as the will is rectified over time, it rests in Christ, not in a careening and obstinate pride. But what if one keeps falling? He must ask for the grace of persevering prayer. Surrendering to God is the true supernatural training of the will. "When you have no wings of prayer to go against the law of gravity, you fall down."[122] Developing a holy hatred of our ego not only saves our soul for eternity but also obtains, even here, peace, union with God, and a foretaste of heaven.

But lastly, what spirit is needed to completely eradicate self-love? Detachment from exterior goods, honors, and riches is needed to complete the purification of the will. One should also not be attached to consolation in prayer, because that is only a means to an end and leads to spiritual pride.[123] Note that adversity is good for us if it comes from God. He loves to see those souls trying to approach Him fight adversity with courage. Victory over or endurance of adversity makes us eager to find the true road and follow it.

Detachment leads to the fruit of peace. And it should be increasing, not diminishing, since the spiritual life accelerates as it moves closer to God. "If thou carry the cross willingly, it will carry thee . . . and will bring thee to thy desired end; namely, to that place where there will be no end."[124]

Now, turn to the prayers to be recited during the *purgative* way and the Chaplet of the Holy Face (p. 15, 20).

---

[122] Bocquet, Fr. Marcel, *The Firebrand*, p. 285.

[123] John of the Cross, *The Ascent of Mount Carmel*, Bk. III, ch. 30, 32.

[124] Thomas à Kempis, *The Imitation of Christ*, Bk. II, ch. 12.

# Day 8

## The Face of Jesus at Nazareth

"Thou shalt hide them in the secret of thy face."[125] What kind of a God art Thou? Thou art simple. For at the same time, Thou art hidden at Nazareth and omnipotent! "O Lord," in Thy hidden life, "shew thy face, and we shall be saved."[126] How much there is to learn by Thy hidden years. Send a ray of Thy hidden Face, which shines with the sweetest peace in the midst of the labors of carpentry, bending over the tools in the wood dust. "I am poor and in labors from my youth: and being exalted have been humbled."[127]

By Jesus being a child, God taught us the great depths of smallness and humility by not only submitting to His heavenly Father but also working under the humble Joseph, His foster father.

What wisdom of God as the Holy Face looked upon Saint Joseph obeying each command and teaching us by example the fourth commandment: honor thy father. The serenity of the Face of the child teaches mankind a lesson: if Jesus lowers Himself infinitely to obey a creature, should we not also obey any superior who gives ordinate commands? No matter how difficult obedience is, Providence gives us support.

Jesus teaches us by living a life of adversity in a poor house. The lesson is clear: adversity[128] makes a battleground of our

---

[125] Ps. 30:21.

[126] Ps.79:20.

[127] Ps. 87:16.

[128] *Ad astra per aspera.* "Through adversity to the stars" is the motto of the state of Kansas. It is a common human understanding that adversity makes natural virtue.

souls in order to wrestle against evil. The victor comes out adorned with virtue.

Go back to Nazareth. The Blessed Virgin Mary, for thirty-three years, never ceased for a moment to glance at the eyes of Jesus, to respond smile with smile. Ah, how she was happier than Saint Veronica, being able, during many years, to render to Him the sacred duty of drying the sweat and dust from His brow.

When life's anxieties crush down upon us, we too can look upon the divine Face and be assured that these burdens may soon become joys and our crosses trophies of victory and salvation.[129]

## The Healing of Pride and Spiritual Sloth

What is the true nature of pride? Pride is the queen and mother of all sin,[130] but lust is a sin of the passions. Saint Thomas mentions that it is less shameful and debasing but more grievous than sins of the flesh because it turns us more away from God.[131] Clergy and religious tend toward pride more than sins of the flesh because the temptations and circumstances of their state lead them down this path. The first sin of the first man was pride.[132] False humility is pernicious because it is a form of hidden pride, more dangerous than that which displays itself and makes itself ridiculous. Pride hides itself all too well because it is opposed to not only humility but also magnanimity. Pride makes one fall into pusillanimity and excessive fear

---

[129] Fourault, *The Month of the Holy Face*, p. 90.

[130] *Summa Theologica* II–II, q. 132, a. 4.

[131] *Summa Theologica* I–II, q. 73, a. 5.

[132] *Summa Theologica* I–II, q. 84. a. 2.

of failure. The pusillanimous fall into the greatest mistake: they do nothing and waste their lives.[133]

In a word, what is pride? It is an inordinate love of our own excellence. The proud man wishes to appear superior to what he really is. Pride focuses on one's own merits and others' insufficiencies; it is a perverse love of greatness;[134] it is a bandage over one's eyes and spirit and hinders in recognizing the majesty of God. It hinders one from asking God for help; thus, God hides His truth from the proud.

What are some different forms of pride? Saint Bernard names a few: curiosity, levity of mind, misplaced joy, singularity, and dissimulation of one's sin in confession.[135] Some take pride in being born into a prominent family, wealth, physical qualities, and one's piety. Intellectual pride can lead to the vice of curiosity, especially the habit of novelty, whereby one acquires inordinate delight in new things.[136]

What are some other defects born of pride? Presumption is the inordinate desire to do what is above one's power. Instead of living out his state in life, he speaks of apostolic zeal and magnanimity but fails in the duty of the little things.

Ambition is the wish to dominate others and govern them without adequate gifts. Vainglory means taking compliments without giving God honor. He is the source of all good. The only "thing" we can own is sin.

What is the remedy for pride? The remedy is to be like Saint Michael, who recognized the majesty due to God. His very

---

[133] Tanquerey, Very Rev. Adolphe, *The Spiritual Life*, no. 1084.

[134] Augustine, *De Civitatae Dei*, Bk. XIV, ch. 13.

[135] Bernard of Clairvaux, *De gradibus humilitatis*, ch. 10.

[136] Ripperger, Fr. Chad, *The Binding Force of Tradition*, p. 45.

name is reparation,[137] "Who is like unto God?" So the remedy is to consider all others greater than oneself because of our hidden faults and others' hidden virtues.[138]

How does one know that he is whittling pride away? It is when he delights not in the praises of men but loves to be unknown and to be esteemed as nothing. "God sweetly reveals His secrets in others and draws him to Himself."[139] But pride cannot be taken away by ourselves: "It is important to realize that all trials are sent or permitted for our purification."[140] It is through adversity that we learn to recognize pride: "What doth he know, that hath not been tried?"[141]

What is the nature of spiritual sloth? This is a dislike of spiritual things or a disgust of piety, which causes one to shorten or omit prayer altogether, rationalizing with vain excuses. Spiritual sloth is the foster parent of lukewarmness.[142]

Acedia[143] is a form of pride because it is an idleness that stifles religious duties necessary for one's sanctification. Spiritual sloth weighs down the soul and crushes it, making the tool of Christ unbearable and the reminder of its duties repulsive. It is not to be confused with passive purification, which is also a weight on the soul but makes the soul ready and strong.[144] Rather, spiritual sloth welcomes distractions to put off the real

---

[137] Reparation in this context means to "repair" the damaged relationship between God and the angelic kingdom.

[138] *Summa Theologica* II–II, q. 161, a. 3.

[139] Thomas à Kempis, *The Imitation of Christ*, Bk. I, ch. 2, 7; Bk. II, ch. 2.

[140] Kevin, Fr., O.C.D., *Way of Perfection for the Laity*, p. 131.

[141] Ecclus. 34:9.

[142] Tanquerey, Very Rev. Adolphe, *The Spiritual Life*, no. 884.

[143] From *acedior*, meaning "to suffer impatiently."

[144] See John of the Cross, *The Dark Night*, Bk. I, ch. 9.

spiritual work, which at times is arduous, in order to embrace laziness and escape. If this goes unchecked, it leads to spiritual anemia, where the world, flesh, and devil become awakened. Beginners in the spiritual life, when God removes His consolation, find their spiritual occupations irksome. This is the very moment a good spiritual director or confessor is needed to coach them through the gap. Spiritual sloth is a mortal sin when one gives up religious duties necessary for salvation, like giving up Mass on Sundays and not making confession when in mortal sin.

What is the cure for spiritual sloth? The sins of the flesh require the tactic of flight,[145] but sloth requires attacking or resisting it. The first step is the hardest, but once it is taken, the second and third, and so on, get progressively easier. One who begins to always think of God not only develops the virtue but also has God answer his prayers. The suggestion is *carpe diem,* "seize the day." Torpor can be resisted by some daily sacrifice to obtain vigor. When sensible devotion is lacking, make reparation for past offenses. Divide the day and make a spiritual rule of life to live by.[146]

Now, turn to the prayers to be recited during the *purgative* way and the Chaplet of the Holy Face (p. 15, 20).

---

[145] To focus on the image of the flesh only makes it worse.

[146] A spiritual rule of life needs to be given to a confessor or spiritual director because everyone is different. Here is an example of a spiritual rule of life. Daily—five decades of the Rosary, fifteen minutes of meditation, ten minutes of spiritual reading, chaplet of the Holy Face. Weekly—Mass three times on top of Sunday. Monthly—day of recollection. Yearly—three-day retreat.

## Day 9

### The Face of Jesus and Satan

"I saw Satan like lightning falling from heaven."[147] Imagine reading these words of Jesus on the edge of a crystal-clear lake in the Rocky Mountains, watching dark clouds forming. After reading this passage, close the Bible; you lift up your eyes and see immediately a clear flash of lightning, and soon, a deep, loud thunderclap. Imagine the Face of Jesus when the sentence was proclaimed on the fallen angels! One moment suffices to cast the enemy of God and of all inordinate love into the abyss.[148]

Jesus was tempted by the devil because He wanted to show us it is through adversity that the soul is led to grow stronger in virtue. Temptation is not a sin, but it can be a blessing in order for one to prove himself in the love of God. Trust is key.

Saint Fernando III was one of the greatest warrior-kings. He fought a constant stream of battles during the Reconquest of Spain. It was because of his deep love and trust in God and Our Lady that God sometimes sent Saint James from heaven to fight the Moors.

How does one vanquish the devil? Grow in the mystical combat of the interior life and look upon Christ the King's Face. He is our warrior in battle, and He will turn His Face on the demons and send the devil disarmed into flight and confusion, just as the Face of the Christ Child looked at the idols of Egypt, and they fell to the ground, not knowing the source of their defeat.[149]

---

[147] Luke 10:18.

[148] Fourault, *The Month of the Holy Face*, p. 95.

[149] Agreda, *The Mystical City of God*, vol. 2, *The Incarnation*, pp. 550–51.

Christ fasting in the desert reminds Christians of the need for mortification. The need for binding and exorcising the demons is still necessary no matter what age. Pope Leo XIII approved of the minor exorcism in the ritual.[150] It is used by exorcists as a diagnostic in demonic cases and deliverance. "Rise up, O Lord, and let Thy enemies be defeated and let all that hate Thee fly before Thy Face."[151] Christians are under the eye of God and should throw themselves on the bosom of the Father. Think of the Face of Jesus in the desert or in the Passion, covered with opprobrium, bleeding and disfigured, and bind the devil in each attack on the soul.

Saint Martin was praying in his cell when a personage appeared with a serene countenance, filled with light, saying, "Martin, I am Christ, adore me." To which he responded, "My Lord Jesus did not announce to me that He would appear to me clad in purple and crowned with a diadem. As for me, if I do not see Him with the Face and exterior beneath which He suffered, with His stigmata and His cross, I will not believe that it is He."[152] At these words, the phantom vanished.

My dear Holy Face of Jesus, teach me how the devil is nothing to fear when Thou are with us. His punishment is to tempt mankind, and by that, one either succumbs to his power or triumphs over his wiles. Thou said Satan fell from heaven like lightning. In all my spiritual combats, I ask that Thou turn Thy Face on the devil and make him melt like wax and go to the foot of the cross to receive his just sentence. Our Lady of the Holy Name of God, protect me from the wiles of the enemy

[150] *Rituale Romanum*, Section XII, Chapter III.

[151] See also Ps. 66:2.

[152] Fourault, *The Month of the Holy Face*, p. 102.

by sweetly saying the Name of Jesus, that Satan's head will be crushed in each battle.

## Sacramental Confession

"Our Lord seeks more our real advantage than our own satisfaction."[153] The majority of souls have a repugnance to making their confession. But it is not consolations that determine our progress, but our dispositions to accept the help of God. "Receive ye the Holy Ghost. Whose sins you shall forgive, they are forgiven them."[154]

How should one prepare for confession? One should examine his conscience, try to have a regular confessor, "counseling him on all the more important manners, even temporal ones; and obey him in everything, especially [one] who is distressed by scruples. He who obeys his confessor need not fear to go astray."[155] Non-frequent penitents need to spend ample time examining their conscience with a traditional guide. Frequent confessors do not require much time.

There are three distinctions: grave sins, more or less deliberate venial sins, and faults of frailty. Mortal sins should be confessed at the beginning by *number*, *kind*, and *cause* or *circumstance*, and with a profound contrition and a purpose to avoid those sins in the future. Any pertinent sins that just do not seem to lose their grip require a desire to atone by an austere life and generous love, like Saint Peter after he denied Jesus, when Jesus looked upon him with His Holy Face.

---

[153] Alphonsus de Liguori, *The Holy Eucharist*, p. 464.

[154] John 20:22–23.

[155] Liguori, St. Alphonsus, *Preparation for Death*, p. 411.

Deliberate venial sins are an obstacle to perfection. They are like poison slowly causing death to the soul and causing it to arrive at a state that cannot resist mortal sin. In reality, they are the second greatest evil to mortal sin.[156] They include sins like petty rancor, inappropriate company with the opposite sex, detraction in small things, rash judgment, and ingratitude to God.

Semi-deliberate venial sins are committed with less reflection and where the soul fights too feebly against them.

Sins of frailty are committed inadvertently because of human weakness. These are very difficult to be completely eradicated, but their number should diminish.

Imperfections are described as choosing lesser real moral good when generosity urges a greater choice. The level of evil of the lesser good depends on its gravity.

How does one confess well? One must desire a great spirit of faith, holding the confessor as Christ. "In frequent confessions stress must be laid on contrition and on the purpose of amendment which necessarily goes with it."[157] We must ask for wisdom to see ourselves as God sees us so we will see all our offenses against God and make a comprehensive accusation.

Saints are attractive, and spiritual writers have written about a certain glow radiating from their faces, like Moses and the Blessed Virgin Mary, to name a couple. That is one reason why they are depicted with a halo. This should motivate us to avoid venial sin because it darkens our intellect and prevents us from the radiating glow emanating from the saints. The

---

[156] Tanquerey, Very Rev. Adolphe, *The Spiritual Life*, no. 726.

[157] Tanquerey, Very Rev. Adolphe, *The Spiritual Life*, no. 266.

motivation to do penance helps one avoid venial sin by rendering charity to God and neighbor.[158]

What are the fruits of confession? The fruits are humility, penance, and absolution. Humility is acted out when kneeling before a priest and accusing oneself of sin. It is a remedy for pride. Heresy, which is a fruit of pride, suppressed confession in the Protestant revolution. Penance allows us to unite ourselves to Christ, who atones for us.[159] "My sin is always before me."[160]

In confession, the Precious Blood of our Redeemer is poured over our soul, not only remitting sins, but enlarging our dispositions of charity. If one falls like Saint Peter at the denial, through intense contrition like his, he may avoid diminishment of progress in the interior life and even go forward after the fall.

Two tips will help those who have little to confess: confess past sins already forgiven in order to rouse greater contrition, and second, ask God to reveal secret sins. One can have moral certitude that sins are forgiven when confessed, but the effects of those sins may still be present. They should cause the soul continued desire to make reparations and greater contrition, which satisfies the debt due to sin.[161]

---

[158] Tanquerey, Very Rev. Adolphe, *The Spiritual Life*, no. 736–734.

[159] Tanquerey, Very Rev. Adolphe, *The Spiritual Life*, no. 742–743.

[160] Ps. l.

[161] For example, a boy hits a ball and breaks his neighbor's window. He asks the neighbor for forgiveness. The neighbor forgives him but tells the boy he owes one hundred dollars to fix the window. The boy labors for the money and satisfies the debt owed in breaking the window. In a similar fashion, God forgives the penitent sinner but requires satisfaction for the debt to sin. Purgatory is the place to do so when it has not been done on this side of eternity.

Saint Veronica of Juliana, a promoter of the Holy Face of Jesus, was told by Him, "Thou shalt make progress in perfection in proportion to the fruits which thou shall draw from this sacrament."[162]

Lastly, no one should ever shirk from confession, for, as Saint Augustine noted, "the penitent should ever grieve and *rejoice* at his grief."[163] We should have sadness: not a vexing sadness but rather a holy sadness. A sadness of contrition for past sins should have sweetness, because that springs from charity. Grieving for sins effects a more intimate union with God because our heart is renewed and a good conscience is restored.[164]

## Assistance at Mass:<br>The Source and Summit of Sanctification

"Can a man," asks Solomon, "hide fire in his bosom, and his garments not burn?"[165] "God is a consuming fire."[166] Why does not the world burn ardently with the fire of the love of God? It is because only a few know the power of the priesthood, the Holy Mass, and Holy Communion. On the cross, Jesus was a bloody immolation, but the Communion of the priest completes the unbloody immolation. The Mass gives grace *ex opere operato*[167] to sinners, so do not resist. Even if a priest is slightly distracted, it cannot stop the grace from coming to a fervent

---

[162] Garrigou-Lagrange, p. 404.

[163] Augustine, *De Poenitentia*, Ch. 13, quoted by Saint Thomas, *Summa Theologica* III, q. 84, a. 9 ad 2um.

[164] Tanquerey, Very Rev. Adolphe, *The Spiritual Life*, no. 743.

[165] Prov. 6:27.

[166] Deut. 4:24.

[167] Meaning "from the work performed."

soul. So the Mass, in effecting grace in the soul, is only limited by obstacles in recipients. When the Good Thief saw the bloody sacrifice of Jesus hanging on the cross, he was moved by such grace that he won heaven by his act of faith, "Lord, remember me when thou shalt come into thy kingdom."[168]

The value of the Mass is thus infinite. Souls should attend daily Mass if their state in life allows them. If not, they should make fervent spiritual communions. Why? The blood of Christ is poured into the soul. But what could have ever induced God to die as a malefactor upon a cross between two sinners, with such insult to His divine majesty? "Who did this?" asks Saint Bernard; he answers,[169] "It was love careless of its dignity."[170]

How should one assist? The Tridentine Mass has many options for assistance. Saint Teresa of Avila, following the ancient monastic patrimony of the Church, gives a hierarchy to forms of prayer, placing vocal prayer as the lowest, meditation in the middle, and contemplation as the highest. One may be attentive to the liturgical prayers, or recall the Passion and Death, pray the Rosary, or continue mental prayer. No matter what level the soul is capable of, it is imperative to unite ourselves profoundly with the oblation of Christ. It behooves the soul to assist at multiple Masses a day, make visits to the Blessed Sacrament, and assist, publicly or privately, at the Divine Office as a way to extend the graces of the Holy Sacrifice throughout the day.

Now, turn to the prayers to be recited during the *purgative* way and the Chaplet of the Holy Face (p. 15, 20).

---

[168] Luke 23:42.

[169] Alphonsus de Liguori, *The Holy Eucharist*, p. 268–69.

[170] *Serm. de Nat. D.*

## Day 10

### The Face of Jesus in the Midst of His Apostolic Career

Imagine the setting sun, a still, glowing globe on the horizon. Our Savior looks with His serene countenance over the steep paths of the mountains of Judah, encompassed in a beautiful setting dusk. He recalls those arid paths where the hot wind blew dust on His sweaty Face. As beads of sweat run down His Sacred Face, He dries them with His handkerchief. Oh, sun, at least veil the splendor of thy ardent beams before Thy Creator!

It is now getting late, and He has not even a stone upon which to lay His head. It has been thirty years of work and prayer which He spent for this, the first days of His public mission—the founding of the Church. He will sleep alone tonight, or will He? He will pray to His Father to send Him apostles. The sweat falls on the parched earth of Israel, sanctifying it to bear fruit. These sweat beads splashed on the ground are not any ordinary seeds—no, they fructify the ground and will not germinate plants, but are the seeds of the fire of the love of God—no, they shall not prove sterile, because the good Shepherd will now begin searching after His rebellious and wandering sheep. The suffering Face of Jesus in the midst of His apostolic career is the source of the power that will ignite the generous souls He is about to meet, like a leaping flame. Once the just and sinners see His Face, they will be riveted onto the path of the Way of Jesus Christ—catching His burning thirst to save souls, which consumes and devours our Most Holy Redeemer. *Sitio!* "I thirst" for the salvation of souls.

Heavenly Redeemer, come visit me with Thy adorable Face. On Thy first day of Thy public mission, Thou sought the apostles and disciples who would pass on Thy doctrine of salvation. But at present, I ask Thee to engender in me an ever-growing and ardent desire to receive Thee in the Most Holy Sacrament of the Altar and to receive the gift of prayer, that infallibly efficacious prayer which prompts me to constantly petition Thy goodness for the graces of my salvation and the salvation of all whom I meet.

## Holy Communion and the Prayer of Petition

"If any man eat of this bread, he shall live forever."[171] The Eucharist is the greatest of sacraments, for it contains not only grace but also the Author of grace. Communion is so called because it ought to foster union of the heart of God and the heart of man, for the virtues of Jesus pass on to the properly disposed soul. Communion always brings on new graces if one is resigned to the suffering and love of the cross.

How does one make a good Communion? Saint Pius X, in 1905, exhorted frequent Communion and to make "a suitable thanksgiving following it."[172] Saint Alphonsus wrote: "Oh, what treasures of grace would you receive, devout soul, if you only entertained yourself with Jesus for an hour, or at least half an hour, after Communion!"[173]

A good intention is necessary for a good Communion, not arising from vanity, custom, or habit, but from the desire to

---

[171] John 6:52.

[172] December 20, 1905.

[173] Alphonsus de Liguori, *The Holy Eucharist*, p. 76.

satisfy the good pleasure of God, to be more closely united to Him in charity, which, if received well, is a remedy of infirmities, defects, and a pledge against mortal sin.

But how does one make a *fervent* Communion? As the preceding sections exhort, if one removes all attachments to venial sin and imperfections, and desires a greater generosity, fervent Communions will happen. The dispositions of humility and profound respect for the Eucharist bring about a great hunger for the Eucharist. Saint Catherine of Siena was so hungry for Holy Communion. Once she "saw the Host in a priest's hand appearing as a globe of fire. The saints were astonished that the hearts of all men were not burned up, and, as it were, reduced to ashes by such a flame.[174] "As Jesus," writes Saint John of Avila, Doctor of the Church, "only came into this world after he had been much and long desired, so does he only enter a soul that desires him."[175]

Each Communion we receive ought to be more fervent than the preceding ones. The saints make more rapid progress at the end of their lives than at the beginning. But if we do not cherish Holy Communion and approach with deep reverence, we can be punished by God, who may take away our religion. We must guard against easy familiarity, or else the situation arises where there are many Communions but with few real communicants. The four ends of sacrifice are petition, adoration, reparation, and thanksgiving. Jesus cured ten lepers, but only one returned to give thanks, and He asked, "Were not ten made clean? and where are the nine?"[176] Is God taking away our religion because our human family is ungrateful? Saint Teresa

[174] Alphonsus de Liguori, *The Holy Eucharist*, p. 283.
[175] Alphonsus de Liguori, *The Holy Eucharist*, p. 70.
[176] Luke 17:17.

said that the thanksgiving is the most precious moment of the spiritual life. Those who dispose themselves allow Christ to speak to them, but they cannot allow for voluntary distraction. Lastly, it is wise to ask the Blessed Virgin Mary to be able to share in her thanksgivings when she was present at the bowing of the head of Jesus on the cross and after her reception of Holy Communion at Saint John's Masses.

Is it necessary to have a strong belief in the efficacy of prayer? Yes. Prayer addresses the mercy of God. The Psalms are filled with these petitions for mercy. True prayer is infallibly efficacious.[177] God has established prayer as a means of salvation.

What is the source of the efficacy of prayer? It comes from the divine will from all eternity, which is as immovable as it is merciful. Some say that prayer will not change the mind of God since He does not change. But this is heresy. True prayer is infallibly efficacious because God has decreed that it should be.[178] "A God who would not have willed and foreseen from all eternity the prayers that we address Him is a conception as puerile as that of a God who would change His plans, bowing before our will."[179] How should we pray?

We cannot pray without being first moved by God because prayer is a participation in God's life, and leads to a desire for perfection and knowledge of God. It perfects and conforms our will to Him.[180] So, if we truly pray for what is necessary for salvation, our hope is that we shall never be lost.

---

[177] *Summa Theologica* II–II, q. 83, a. 15 and 2um.

[178] *Summa Theologica* II–II, q. 83, a. 2.

[179] Garrigou-Lagrange, *The Three Ages of the Interior Life*, vol. 1, p. 431.

[180] Tanquerey, Very Rev. Adolphe, *The Spiritual Life*, no. 499.

We should petition for final perseverance because it can never be merited, but it only comes through humble, trusting, and *persevering* prayer. "A person should begin to pray solely to please God, that is, solely to learn what the will of God is in his regard and to beg of Him the help to put it into practice."[181]

Be assured that if we truly keep praying, it shows God is helping us, for without actual grace, we would not continue to pray. God loves to allow adversity to visit us because, by means of struggle, we learn to love to battle for God. "My grace is sufficient for thee: for power is made perfect in infirmity."[182] God bestows upon us innumerable benefits unasked, unsought, but there are some which He will grant only at our request.[183] So we should petition God for growth in the interior life and the prayer of union. But we must do so in humility and trust, knowing that all good comes from God.

Now, turn to the prayers to be recited during the *purgativ*e way and the Chaplet of the Holy Face (p. 15, 20).

## Day 11

### The Holy Face of Jesus Praying to His Father before Calling the Disciples

The Holy Face opens His eyes after only a few hours of sleep under the stars. He kisses the ground and kneels when He addresses His heavenly Father. "I wish to glorify Thee on earth and begin the work with which Thou give me to do. I will

---

[181] Alphonsus de Liguori, *The Holy Eucharist*, p. 344.

[182] 2 Cor. 12:9.

[183] Tanquerey, Very Rev. Adolphe, *The Spiritual Life*, no. 509.

manifest Thy name to those who Thou will give me and many will keep Thy name. I pray for them: I pray not for the world, but for them whom Thou will give me: because they are Thine. . . . Holy Father keep them in Thy name whom Thou will give Me; that, they may be one, as We also are."[184]

He stops speaking and looks upon the full moon. What does Jesus think? Does He recall His Mother, the Blessed Virgin Mary? Is she keeping vigil now and praying for Jesus on His first night of mission? Does He pray to all the guardian angels of the future apostles and disciples? Does He send them each a special message and a picture of His luminous Face into their minds, a gentle look with many darts of grace, a smile that awakens their slumber and a spark of unique joy—is the Messiah among us?

Jesus gets up and approaches the city. He will encounter His first people on His unique mission to establish the Way—the first Christians. His Father received His prayer and will answer by giving our human race the Church, over which the gates of hell shall never prevail.

Dear Christian, did Jesus also pray for you, that you may be one with Him and with the Father? In whatever situation you find yourself—the Church enduring her passion, or the Church enjoying her triumph, or the Church surviving the end time—what is your response? For beginners, it is to begin mental prayer. For the proficient, it is to continue the progressive prayer of the simple. For the perfect, it is to maintain a life of prayer and persevere in it.

[184] Cf. John 17:4, 6, 9, 11.

## Prayer of Venerable Leo DuPont[185]

O Almighty God, Father Eternal, look on the Face of Thy Son Jesus; we present it to Thee with confidence to implore our pardon. Merciful advocate, He opens His mouth to plead our cause; listen to His cries, behold His tears, oh my God, and because of His infinite merits, listen to Him when He intercedes for us, poor and miserable sinners. Amen.

## Mental Prayer for Beginners: How to Attain a Life of Prayer and Persevere in It

What is active participation at Mass, at our Rosary, at our Holy Hour? It is making contact with the Most Holy Trinity, who is full act Himself. The Blessed Trinity dwells within, and it is necessary to be quiet so the light will come to our recollection. The greatest things of the Church start with contemplation. Jesus started the Church after thirty years of obscurity. The more one prays like Jesus, the Blessed Virgin Mary, and the saints, with meekness and humility, the more intimate is mental prayer. Saint Teresa says that mental prayer is friendship with God and frequently conversing in secret with Him.[186] One of Saint John Marie Vianney's parishioners told him, "I look at our Lord who is in the tabernacle, and He looks at me." Simplicity is the key to prayer, not complicated methods. A method may help one in order to acquire convictions or to strengthen them from mental ramblings. Prayer depends on God's grace, and those who are faithful in their duties

---

[185] The Apostle of the Holy Face (January 24, 1797–January 18, 1876) was a Catholic layman who was declared venerable by Pope Pius XII. He was a friend to Sr. Marie de St. Pierre and found the relics of Saint Martin of Tours which were buried by the French Revolution.

[186] Teresa of Avila, *Life*, ch. 8.

and the small things are given the gift of prayer. Prayer is most helpful for attainment of salvation and perfection.[187]

Love of knowledge without the love of God is not prayer; it only increases pride. Prayer begins and ends in the love of God. The generous soul is like the sailor who puts up the sails, but the Holy Ghost provides the wind. In other words, the soul does not go without God's assistance.

Normally we should begin prayer with one act of humility. For example, with the intention of union with the Incarnate Word to render through Him the religious homage due to God and reproduce in ourselves the virtues of Jesus Christ.[188] After this, what acts are to be made? Recall God, His goodness, truth, beauty, and simplicity: Christ and the mysteries of His life; our duties, vocation, sin, death, judgment, heaven, and hell. A few words either read or recalled from the Bible or the liturgy can "kick start" the prayer.

Remember the devil sows interference. But at the very moment of arriving on the cusp of mental prayer, the soul does well to allow prayer to pierce through his armor in order to gaze with faith on the goodness of God. This act of valor engenders adoration, Jesus before our eyes; communion, Jesus in our heart, cooperation, Jesus in our hands. This leads us to form a resolution for greater fidelity. [189] When thinking of sin, ask the good God to break us from all slavery to sin. Pray the Our Father very slowly, only one verse at a time, followed by a savoring of it. "I will it," meaning, "I will God's plan." Bask in submitting to His plan, because it is better than the alternative.

---

[187] Tanquerey, Very Rev. Adolphe, *The Spiritual Life*, no. 669.
[188] Tanquerey, Very Rev. Adolphe, *The Spiritual Life*, no. 697.
[189] Tanquerey, Very Rev. Adolphe, *The Spiritual Life*, no. 699.

## The Prayer of Simplicity

If one used a method at the beginning, it should give way to a simple gaze, a just *being with* God, like Mary being at the feet of Jesus. "The prayerful soul does little and receives much."[190] A simple gaze on God or the Face of Jesus Christ is all that is needed, not reasoning, discourse, or affections. We were made for union, and the simpler it is, the greater it is. The simple gaze on Jesus requires little and will receive much.

The simple gaze comes with a price. Great purity of heart, true mortification, and death to self are a few traits. But so few desire these means, and that is why so few advance in it. Consider sufferings as the currency to obtain the prayer of simplicity. After the necessary purgation of soul, which gives all to God, comes to pass, then rest, joy, and illumination are given as a means to union with God. This is called the passive purification of the senses.

How does one attain a life of prayer? Ask God for the humility to be like little children held in His arms. We should love contempt because God is who is, and we are nothing and deserving of contempt. We need to be mortified of the world, or we will always be preoccupied with petty jealousies, memory of wrongs, rash judgments, and be unable to converse with our Lord. In the course of the day, we should find ourselves having a constant conversation with God and not ourselves. We must create silence in the soul because Elijah only heard God in the quiet whisper. If the soul is generous, Jesus will help the soul pacify the senses so they will submit to the higher regions of the soul. When a soul constantly reads, listens, or attends to

---

[190] Tanquerey, Very Rev. Adolphe, *The Spiritual Life*, no. 1364.

good spiritual things, this remote preparation helps her know the subject matter of the prayer. For example, assisting at the Mass commemorating the event of the translation of the Holy House of Loreto can give the soul images of the flying house of Nazareth as the subject of its prayer. The event of the translation of the Holy House, which was the scene of the Annunciation, was witnessed by farmers in its flight before it settled in current day Loreto, Italy. Also, fidelity to the present moment is paramount. Do not let the devil make you inordinately think about the past or the future. We can do nothing about it. This way of thinking is one of his favorite traps. We can only become a saint *now* because God is the eternal now.

How does one persevere? One must make the prayer of simplicity a way of life. This is done because God is glorified during the entire day. This habitual loving gaze makes God better known and loved. We forget self and creatures because we know God more deeply. Life becomes a protracted act of religion.[191]

To persevere, it is necessary to have confidence in God. Let Him lead. We should stop leading ourselves apart from Him, for He is the Good Shepherd who leads His sheep as He judges best. If we are visited with aridity, this is the path the Lord has chosen for us. It is like the fire that must dry out the wood before setting it ablaze. The sensible appetites must submit to the spirit. The egoist always thinks about himself. But the wise man thinks of the glory of God and allows even painful events to be seen in the light of the supreme goodness of God.

Now, turn to the prayers to be recited during the *purgative* way and the Chaplet of the Holy Face (p. 15, 20).

---

[191] Tanquerey, Very Rev. Adolphe, *The Spiritual Life*, no. 1370.

# Middle Theme: Illuminative Way of Proficients

## Prayers to Be Recited During the Illuminative Way

### Litany of the Holy Face

*Taken from the Scriptures*

Lord, have mercy on us.
Jesus Christ, have mercy on us.

Lord, have mercy on us.
Jesus Christ, hear us.
Jesus Christ, graciously hear us. God the Father, who art in Heaven, **have pity on us**.
God, the Son, Redeemer of the world,

God, the Holy Ghost,
Holy Trinity, one God,

Jesus, who didst take on Thyself the form of a servant,
Jesus, who didst converse with men,
Jesus, who didst weep over Jerusalem,
Jesus, whose Face didst shine like the sun,
Jesus, who didst prostrate Thyself upon Thy Face,

**have pity on us.**

Jesus, whose Face was bathed in a bloody sweat,
Jesus, betrayed by the kiss of Judas,
Jesus, who didst receive a blow from the hand of a servant,
Jesus, whose Face was veiled,
Jesus, whose Face was covered with spittle,
Jesus, whose Face was wounded with blows,
Jesus, crowned with thorns,
Jesus, whose head was struck with a reed,
Jesus, whose Face commands a reverent silence over the whole earth,
Jesus, who dost show Thy face above Thy sanctuary,
Jesus, before whose Face we utter our prayers,
Jesus, from whose Face we expect mercy,

Jesus, from whose Face none of our doings are hidden,
Jesus, whose Face causes the mountains to melt away,
Jesus, who didst not turn Thy Face away from spittings,

Jesus, who didst present Thy cheeks to those who struck Thee,
Jesus, who was looked upon as a leper,

Jesus, whose Face we behold with joy,
Jesus, whose eyes observe those who do evil,
Jesus, who causest to shine upon us the light of Thy Face,
Jesus, whose head is of most pure gold,
Jesus, whose lips distill an excellent myrrh,

**have pity on us.**

Jesus, in whose eyes the heavens are not pure,[192]
Jesus, on whose lips grace is shed,
Jesus, whose eyes are witnesses of our tears,
Jesus, whose Face rejoices the just,
Jesus, whose eyes are attentive to the poor,
Jesus, whose eyes are upon those that fear Thee,
Jesus, whose eyes behold the just,
Jesus, whose eyes are upon the faithful on the earth,
Jesus, whose eyes resemble those of a dove,

Jesus, whose eyes are like a burning lamp,
Jesus, whose eyes are like a flaming fire,
Jesus, whose eyes are more brilliant than the sun,
Jesus, whose eyes rest upon those that love Thee,
Be merciful unto us, pardon us Jesus.

} **have pity on us.**

From all evil, **deliver us, Jesus.**

From sudden and unprovided death,

From eternal damnation,
By the mystery of Thy holy Incarnation,
By Thy glorious Transfiguration,
By Thy tears,
By the blows Thou didst receive,

By Thy crown of thorns,
At the day of judgment,

} **deliver us, Jesus.**

We sinners, **we beseech Thee, hear us.**
That being dead to sin, we may live to justice,
**we beseech Thee, hear us.**

---

[192] Job xv: 15 "Behold among his saints none is unchangeable, and the heavens are not pure in his sight."

Having suffered in the flesh, arm us with the same thought,
**we beseech Thee, hear us.**
Grant that we may apply ourselves to know nothing,
save Jesus crucified, **we beseech Thee, hear us.**
Having taken part in Thy sufferings grant us a share
in Thy consolations, **we beseech Thee, hear us.**
Grant us to see Thee, Face to face, in heaven,
**we beseech Thee, hear us.**

Son of God, hear us.

Lamb of God, who takest away the sins of the world,
**spare us, Jesus.**
Lamb of God, who takest away the sins of the world,
**graciously hear us, Jesus.**
Lamb of God, who takest away the sins of the world,
**have mercy on us, Jesus.**

## *Antiphon*

Oh God, the whole earth is troubled when anger shows itself on Thy Face; but, oh Lord our God, grant unto us mercy, and do not proceed to the last extremity;[193] show us Thy Face and we shall be saved.

V. Let God arise, and let His enemies be scattered.

R. And let all who hate Him, flee from before His Face.

---

[193] The "last extremity" may be exacting the anger and wrath of Divine justice.

*Prayer*

Almighty and merciful God, grant, we beseech Thee, that whilst reverencing the Face of Thy Christ, disfigured in the Passion because of our sins, we may merit to contemplate it, shining forever in celestial glory. Through the same Jesus Christ. Amen.

## Prayer to Entreat for the Triumph of the Church by Means of the Holy Face

*Taken from the Scriptures*

*(Dan. 11:13, 14, 17, 18, 19)*

Lord, we entreated not Thy Face, that we might turn from our iniquities and think on Thy truth. And the Lord hath watched upon the evil and hath brought it upon us: the Lord our God is just in all His works which He hath done: for we have not harkened to His voice. Now, therefore, O God, hear the supplication of Thy servant and his prayers: and shew Thy Face upon Thy sanctuary which is desolate, for Thy own sake. Incline, O my God, Thy ear and hear; open Thy eyes and see our desolation, and the city upon which Thy Name is called: for it is not for our justifications that we present our prayers before Thy Face, but for the multitude of Thy tender mercies. O Lord, hear: O Lord, be appeased: harken and do: delay not for Thy own sake, O my God, because Thy Name is invocated upon Thy city and upon Thy people. But there is no one who invokes this powerful Name; there is none who lifts himself up to Thee and who endeavours by his supplications to restrain the effects of Thy anger. Therefore, Thou hast turned away Thy Face from us, and Thou hast bruised us under the weight of our iniquities. Lord, look upon us in pity, keep no longer silent, and do not leave us prey to such sharp sorrows. Oh! if Thou wouldst open the heavens and come down! The mountains would tremble before Thy Face. Thy Name would be known amongst Thy enemies, the nations would be struck with terror. Cast Thy eyes upon us, and remember that we are Thy people. Amen.

## Day 12

### The Holy Face and Magdalen

There was a woman of great renown in the city, and this woman was a sinner.[194]

It was a fresh morning with the spring wind, and Saint Mary Magdalen was strolling around her house. What was running through her mind? Her conscience was pricking her peace. *The people of town know that I am a sinner, that I love the attention of men, but without my sin, how else could I be independent?*

Behold, a multitude is passing by, and one of them is a prophet. They were hanging on every word of Jesus. "I say to you that even so there shall be joy in heaven upon one sinner that does penance."[195] These words fall onto her ears and a great peace comes upon her. "Was that," she thinks, "meant for me?" Yes, and for each of us sinners. Then Jesus raises His head, and His divine eyes meet with Mary's. They smile. "The glance of the Divine Face met the glance of the sinner."[196]

---

[194] See Luke 7:37. *Mullier in civitate peccatrix.*

[195] Luke 15:7.

[196] Fourault, *The Month of the Holy Face*, p. 117.

Then she is caught in adultery. But as she is about to be stoned, Jesus arrives. "He who is without sin, cast the first stone."[197] Jesus writes in the dust the sins of all present. Mary raises her dust-filled face and looks at the Savior's Face. She is forever now a disciple.

Then she comes to a house some days later and looks upon the Face of Jesus. She takes the alabaster jar and anoints His feet and washes them with her hair and tears.

Later, she goes alongside Our Lady of Dolors at the foot of the cross. Her tears are streaming as the onlookers blaspheme the dying Jesus. Does she flee? No, a flash of grace moves her to look at the Face of our dying Savior, and He consoles her.

She helps bury Jesus and returns the next day to the tomb. The sinner is one of the first to encounter the singular grace of receiving the look of the resurrected Holy Face.

Dear soul, how do we have the assurance to do the same? Imitate the sinner turned to saint. On her knees, at His feet, she listened, contemplated, and adored. "Mary has chosen the better part, and it shall not be taken away from her."[198]

Dear Holy Face of Jesus, look on me as a sinner. Every other soul is greater than me because of my hidden faults and their hidden virtues. Never again look away from me due to my sins, but look at me like Thou did at Saint Mary Magdalen, *peccatrix*, and bring down Thy grace into my soul so that I go through the second conversion and persevere through its dark night, knowing that Thou will always be beside me, my hope and confidence.

---

197 See John 8:7.

198 Luke 10:42.

# The Second Conversion, Its Passive Purification, and Conduct to Be Observed in this Night of the Senses

What is the first conversion? It is Baptism. It is the removal of original sin.[199] Yet, if the soul falls after Baptism, it is living in mortal sin until it returns to the state of grace after a good confession.

But those who are in the state of grace need a second conversion. What is the second conversion? It is becoming like a little child held in the arms of our Father. "Amen I say to you, unless you be converted and become as little children, you shall not enter into the kingdom of heaven."[200] This conversion requires a greater humility, which is found in the purgative way, a consciousness of total dependence on God and the soul's own weakness. When the disciples were entertaining thoughts of who amongst them was the greatest, Jesus said, "Let him become as the younger."[201] For example, Saint Peter's first conversion was when he left his fishing and went to follow Jesus. But Jesus prayed for Peter that he would one day be strong enough to confirm the brethren. He needed a second conversion with his whole heart. Saint John of the Cross calls this second conversion the passive purification of the senses, since it marks the entrance into the illuminative way.

How is the second conversion shown in the lives of the servants of God? Fr. Charles Lallement[202] mentions that the first

---

[199] And actual sin for those who are baptized after the age of reason and have committed sin before Baptism.

[200] Matt. 18:3.

[201] Luke 22:26.

[202] Fr. Charles Lallement (1578–April 5, 1635) was a French Jesuit. Author of *La Doctrine Spirituelle*, he saw the importance of the contemplative life over the active life and taught the Jesuits in formation its high ideals.

is when they devote themselves to the service of God, and the second is when they give themselves entirely to perfection. For the apostles, it was marked by the descent of the Holy Ghost.[203]

But because of their own negligence, not all priests or religious pass through the second conversion. The second conversion should come in the third year of the novitiate and/or major orders for the clerical state. Purity of heart is required to receive the graces here. To pass this stage well and to persevere in it is a great sign of merit.

Why is it necessary to go through the second conversion? Because before it, the soul has a mercenary love of God. In other words, it is selfish and looks for some temporal benefit while in God's service. Before, the soul expresses an inordinate self-love. Father Lallement says that before the second conversion, the soul only follows its nature and human sense in practically everything, paying little attention to the inspirations of the Holy Ghost. These people lead their lives by the example of others who themselves are imperfect. One will never go through the second conversion unless he looks to the Holy Ghost for guidance.

People tend toward natural activity instead of supernatural because, "mental prayer is real hard work, especially for beginners."[204] Only prayer can protect us from this delusion, according to Father Lallement.

Therefore, it is necessary to do everything it takes to pass through the dark night. This makes an interior man who, when he speaks, makes a much greater impression in a few words than the verbose man who utilizes only a straining of the reason and

---

[203] Lallement, *La Doctrine Spirituelle*, 2nd principle, ch. 6, 2.2, p. 113.

[204] Chautard, Dom Jean-Baptiste, O.C.S.O., *The Soul of the Apostolate*, p. 200.

study. The former begins to live heaven now, enjoying a constant conversation with God.

Saint Catherine of Siena, in her *Dialogue*, speaks of the second conversion. Souls are nothing without God. But in adversity, the soul flies to God alone with true humility; meanwhile, God withdraws His consolation but not His grace. Saint Peter's fall is a good analogy, "Woman, I know him not."[205] When Jesus looked upon Peter, Peter grew in charity. Saint Catherine says that every perfection proceeds from and is nourished by charity, and charity is nourished by humility. Peter had a holy hatred of self, "hiding himself in his own house . . . [he] began to weep."[206] But he and the apostles were imperfect until Pentecost, for they were in fear, barring themselves in the upper room, "because the soul always fears until it arrives at love."[207]

Fr. Johannes Tauler[208] expresses a climax in the life of the soul to illustrate this second conversion, stating that when a man is plunged into his anxiety, he either becomes aware of the pursuit of God or he does not. In the former, Jesus comes into the soul, "He takes him by the hand; and while he has one foot in hell and the other outside, He still preaches to him, He implored him not to abuse His graces."[209]

---

205 Luke 22:57.

206 Catherine of Siena, *Dialogue*, ch. 63.

207 Catherine of Siena, ch. 63.

208 Father Johannes Tauler (c. 1300–June 16, 1361) was a German Dominican priest and a mystic. He believed that the state of the soul was affected more by a personal relationship with God than by external practices.

209 St. Leonard of Port Maurice, "The Little Number of Those Who are Saved."

What should a soul do when pursued by God? Cry like the woman of Canaan: "Have mercy on me, O Lord."[210] Saint John of the Cross thinks this is the moment when the soul enters the contemplative life. And this is when God removes His consolation, like Jesus does when He appears not to hear the questions of the woman of Canaan. But this withdrawal of God is for the advantage of the soul because it increases perseverance, confidence in God, and zeal. To sum it up, when pursued by God, desire what He wants, nothing more, nothing less!

But until Christ reigns in the soul, He continues to pursue, so give in to His Majesty.

Why is this conversion necessary? "Great purity of heart is required for contemplation. Now even advanced souls are subject to many imperfections and experience, though in a milder form, a reawakening of the seven capital sins."[211]

According to Saint John of the Cross, three signs of the second conversion are manifested:

1. No comfort in the things of God, and none in created things.
2. The memory dwells ordinarily upon God, with painful anxiety and thinks it no longer serves Him.
3. The inability to meditate and make reflection.[212]

Why does this happen? God gives a grace that is purely spiritual and not sensual; it is a higher form of life. It hurts because God is nearer than before, and nothing could be more opposite than

[210] Matt. 15:22.

[211] Tanquerey, Very Rev. Adolphe, *The Spiritual Life*, no. 1420.

[212] John of the Cross, *The Dark Night of the Soul*, Bk. I, ch. 9.

God and a soul needing purgation of sin. Sometimes, according to Saint Augustine, the gift of tears accompanies the soul, as with Saint Peter after his denial. The soul penetrates beyond formulas of the faith to an experiential knowledge of self and one's miseries, a purer and truer knowledge of God, curing of the capital sins in their more refined form. In summary, these aridities make a soul advance in pure love of God and only wishes to please Him.[213]

What conduct is to be observed in the dark night of the senses called the second conversion? One must not abandon prayer or get discouraged. Get a good spiritual director or a holy confessor to guide you. Accelerate the period by humility, abnegation, and trust in God. The chief disposition . . . is that of holy abandonment to God: they must kiss the Hand that strikes them, that they have indeed merited these trials . . .[214] "Spiritual writers tell us that this period may extend two to fifteen years."[215]

Now, a keener generosity is necessary because a man is at the aurora of the illuminative state. The seven capital sins are being burnt, and any pain draws greater merit; otherwise, the same purification in purgatory happens without merit.

In a word, trust in God and give a simple, loving gaze to the Holy Face of Jesus and Mary, do not desire consolation, say the Our Father slowly. You are beginning a new life, and you will be out of your comfort zone, but in the silence of Mass or conversation with Our Lady, God will give short inspirations

---

[213] See Tanquerey, Very Rev. Adolphe, *The Spiritual Life*, no. 1428–1431.
[214] Ibid., 1432.
[215] Ibid., 1432.

that will stay with you for a while because He is speaking to you on a higher level.

What should the souls be aware of? Emptiness of created things and temptations against chastity and patience are usual trials. God uses these as a means to strengthen the virtues affecting the sense appetite. Temptations can be a blessing here because it obliges one to pray. This gives the soul an awareness of its own vileness and the majesty of God. Lastly, this grace effects in the soul a more lively charity and more spontaneous knowledge of God and a greater confidence in prayer.

Now, turn to the prayers to be recited during the *illuminative* way and the Chaplet of the Holy Face (p. 85, 20).

## Day 13

### The Kiss of the Holy Face Bestowed on Little Children

The Gospel scenes of Jesus and the little children approaching Him are portrayed in paintings. One infant stands at a distance with his arms outstretched to Jesus. Some children are hugging Him as He preaches to the mothers. The rays of Jesus's innocent Face attract the attention of this cherished portion of the flock. He kisses the faces of these little lambs.

Why does Jesus show such great interest in His innocent ones? Because He Himself is innocent and simple. He helps one who can rest in His arms. He is looking at you, dear reader, so become little like one of these if you wish to enter the kingdom of heaven.

The disciples asked Jesus who would be the greatest in heaven. He told them to be innocent and simple like doves. Jesus exhorts spiritual childhood over spiritual pride. Because charity is not ambitious or competitive, and it does not rejoice in iniquity. Childlike simplicity has a certain holy forgetfulness of self. Jesus taught in parables, and the wise of the world did not understand their inner meaning. But it is the childlike, not to be confused with the childish, who are the ones who advance in the spiritual life as proficients. Proficients are humble, esteeming themselves as little to make room for our Savior to be their rock. They are the clean of heart who do not scandalize the children whose angels always see the Face of His Father. "With what care He warded off the crowd in order to let the children approach Him."[216]

So be a dove and be a child, and the Good Shepherd will draw you with His gentle staff into His arms. "He that loveth cleanness of heart shall have the king as his friend."[217] "Blessed are the clean of heart, for they shall see God."[218]

O my dear Redeemer, lover of the little ones, allow me to gaze with the look of an innocent child upon the becoming rays of Thy Holy Face. May it strengthen me to continue the next stage of the spiritual mountain of Sion. As I climb, or rather, as Thou lifts me up like a spiraling eagle ever higher, may the parables and the mysteries of the Rosary be a movement where eternal life begins in my bosom as a foretaste of the upper courts of the New Jerusalem.

---

[216] Fourault, *The Month of the Holy Face*, p. 128.

[217] Prov. 22:11.

[218] Matt. 5:8.

## The Spiritual Age of Proficients and Prudence in the Interior Life

The illuminative way of proficients, contrasted with the purgative way of beginners, has certain marks, just as adolescence contrasted with childhood. The proficient soul is less imaginative and more rational. Previously, the soul knew God, but only a little, in the Divine Liturgy and public prayer, but the proficient actively carves out a spiritual rule of life, recalling the presence of God without the aid of external sources.

The proficient prays the Rosary every day, not just repeating the mysteries on the surface, but penetrating them in light of their salvific value. Sin becomes the only object of grief, and the soul begins to make spontaneous prayers, begging God to take all sin away.

The soul should become more in touch with the Church Militant, Church Suffering, and Church Triumphant. She develops conversations with the Communion of Saints and develops a desire to read their beautiful lives. The love of the cross grows, engendering a greater strength to carry it. The parables of the Gospel and lessons from life are seen in a more penetrating way such that the soul moves spirally, like an eagle soaring to the sun in which eternal life begins, remaining out of the state of mortal sin.

There is more or less contemplation depending on the fidelity and generosity of the soul. The understanding of God and His Church is more penetrating because the soul is more pure and childlike.

At this age, God conquers the intellect, and the soul lets Him because the proficient is not puffed up with worldly knowledge but rather sees the vanity of the world, a true knowledge of good and evil, which is a reversal of the words of the serpent in the garden.[219] God rewards the generosity of the soul with a certain docility and freedom. He gives it lights that are often scarcely perceived: commonsense, a habit of reflection, readiness to consult others, determination, foresight, and caution.[220] This superior simplicity allows the soul to make the loving gaze upon the Holy Face more frequent. Precise formulas, if used previously, will begin to be abandoned—for the soul is on a higher ground.

Spiritual reading is no longer a set of formulas to study but a sweet interior life upon which to grow. The truths of the Holy Mass are sufficient for the soul to grow, who sees its import as "the study of Our Lords' actions and words as set forth in the Gospel."[221]

What is the love of God in the souls of the proficient? They move from the battle of overcoming mortal sin and practice the love of conformity with the Divine Will by obeying God's commandments.[222] They desire to consider chastity, obedience, and poverty as a way of life, or to live by their spirit, and a keenness for the kingdom of God to come and the salvation of souls develops.

> In such a life the soul loves God, no longer only "with its whole heart" in the midst of sensible consolation, but "with all its soul," with all its activities, not yet however "with all its strength," as will happen in the night of the spirit, nor as yet "with all its mind," for the soul is not yet

---

[219] "And you shall be as Gods knowing good and evil" (Gen. 3:5).

[220] Tanquerey, Very Rev. Adolphe, *The Spiritual Life*, no. 1428–1034.

[221] Tanquerey, Very Rev. Adolphe, *The Spiritual Life*, no. 1428–1033.

[222] Tanquerey, Very Rev. Adolphe, *The Spiritual Life*, no. 1428–1226.

> established in this superior region. That it may be established there, true passive purification of the higher part of the soul will be needed, a purification that brings about the disappearance of all spiritual and intellectual pride which still mingles in the faculty for prayer and action.[223]

What is the spiritual edifice of proficients? Now that the soul rarely, if ever, falls into mortal sin, it now has the peace for Jesus to build a spiritual edifice. The rock is Christ, and the base is humility. The pillars of faith and hope support the cupola[224] of charity. The edifice has two doors, with the gifts of counsel, piety, fortitude, and fear of God supported by the cardinal (hinges) virtues of prudence, justice, fortitude, and temperance. Lastly, the lamps of the gifts of wisdom, understanding, and knowledge burn inside.

Why is prudence important in the interior life? Prudence is best explained by its contrary defects. The foolish virgins were not prudent enough to have oil to burn when the bridegroom arrived. They were figuratively locked out of heaven.[225] What should one avoid? First, avoid lack of consideration and rash haste in judgment. Give time to prayerfully discern difficult or important decisions. Second, avoid slyness and cunning, which are ordered to lower goods.

Lack of consideration wants to hasten spiritual growth, but instead impedes it. One who tries to advance too hastily and does not move with the speed of the Holy Ghost falls on his face. These like to harvest the flowers of the tree prematurely instead of letting the fruit mature.

---

223 Garrigou-Lagrange, p. 70–71.

224 A domed roof.

225 See Matt. 25:4.

What is required of prudence? It means doing the right thing at the right time in the right way. It uses natural reason to preserve us from impulsiveness and not to follow our whims or sensible appetites.

What is infused prudence? It is a great virtue and superior to justice, fortitude, and temperance, the other moral virtues. It is not a negative prudence which is against the undertaking of great things. It also does not mean to aim at the mediocre. "But the wisdom that is from above, first indeed is chaste, then peaceable, modest, easy to be persuaded, consenting to the good, full of mercy and good fruits, without judging, without dissimulation."[226] Infused prudence ranks immediately below faith, hope, and charity. Many theologians say that Christian prudence is exceedingly rare. This prudence should grow with charity, and the soul should begin to see the supernatural over the natural the more it progresses.

What is holy discretion? It gives the soul to see importance of the little things in Christian life. It renders to the soul a gratitude for the graces received, born a child of wrath and that God owes him nothing; whereas indiscreet souls rob the honor due to God.[227] Discretion helps a soul never to act without previous reflection. Thus, the habit of deciding nothing, of doing nothing that is not referred to God, is gradually acquired.[228]

What happens when discretion is enlightened by the gift of counsel? It becomes simple like a dove and remains silent when it ought and speaks only from truth when silence must give place to words. This gift is evident when difficult or unforeseen

[226] James iii, 13–18.

[227] Catherine of Siena, *Dialogue*, ch. IX.

[228] Tanquerey, Very Rev. Adolphe, *The Spiritual Life*, no. 1428–1032.

circumstances occur. Saint Athanasius was evading the Arians who were threatening his life. He left through the back door of his cathedral and got on a boat on the Nile. His pursuers followed in a boat behind him. Saint Athanasius hid behind in a cove, exchanged his cassock for secular clothing, and then sailed toward his persecutors. When they met, they asked, "Have you seen Athanasius?" Athanasius responded, "He is near." The gift of counsel gave him the ability to remain truthful while still keeping him from his pursuers.

Now, turn to the prayers to be recited during the *illuminative* way and the Chaplet of the Holy Face (p. 85, 20).

# Day 14

## The Holy Face and Lazarus

And when He drew nigh to the tomb, He wept. Notice the Holy Face of Jesus streaming with tears as He interiorizes, in His Sacred Humanity, the death of His dear friend Lazarus. Notice the onlookers as Jesus approached His beloved friend, "Behold how he loved him."[229]

Thy tears, dear Jesus, show me how dear and precious Thou art. How many tears are shed to overpower sinners who are about to die the second death of sin and eternal perdition? How many Marthas and Marys shed tears for their loved ones today over the tomb of impenitent sinners? Remove them from the tomb of their sins and command them, "Wake up poor sinners!"

---

[229] John 11:36.

Could not have Jesus prevented the death of Lazarus? Yes, but it was needful that God should be glorified. When the last hour strikes and the death toll finds me in the extremity of my last illness, taking away the heat from my limbs, behold, the Holy Face will look upon me as He did, bitterly weeping in front of the tomb of Lazarus. That divine look will remind me that the shadow of this life, the valley of tears, is soon to pass, and I am to be resurrected like Lazarus on my final day, supported by the sacraments of Holy Mother the Church and the gift of piety in my filial affection toward God as a very loving Father.

Yes, Jesus wept in this valley of tears, as do all Christian souls who patiently suffer injustice. But, "I am the resurrection and the life."[230] Be brave, dear Christian souls, as Jesus was brave to enter into the public after having just escaped stoning. We have one life to live. How will our funeral look? What will people say of us? Hopefully, "Behold how he loved him."[231] Our Savior loved those who imitated Him in virtue. Lazarus must have been a just man, giving to each his due. He must have been patient and meek, with the flowing of charity. He must have been chaste above all, adding his spiritual fruitfulness. Saints are attractive, and Jesus was attracted to the beautiful lives of Martha, Mary, and Lazarus.

Oh my Redeemer, Thou are the Good Shepherd that uses Thy rod to free us from the thorns of sin. Look upon me with that look Thou had in front of the tomb of Lazarus. When I am entangled in the midst of sin, shed a ray of Thy merciful Holy Face and awake me from its shackles. When Thou hast

---

[230] John 11:25.

[231] John 11:36.

redeemed me, never let me be separated from Thy Divine gaze again. Support me with the graces of a just heart, a chaste heart, and a meek heart like Thine, as I turn my back on sin and turn my face unreservedly upon Thy Holy Face.

## Christian Justice, Patience, and Meekness

Many pious souls do not consider the importance of justice. Saint John of the Cross suffered prison and many injustices from his religious brethren. When justice is practiced more rigorously, it helps the soul be emptied of egoism. Justice is found in the will. Thus, doing good and avoiding evil makes for a sound will. When a very just man is noticed by others, they say that he is a very good man. The Ten Commandments deal with justice: the first three, giving to God His due, and the last seven, giving to neighbor his due.

Commutative justice governs exchanges and forbids stealing. Distributive justice means sharing goods, works, duties, and rewards among the population for the common good. Equity not only considers the letter of the law but the spirit governing it in a Christian way.

The value of justice is made known by one who suffers from injustice. Breaking the Ten Commandments is a good summary of what injustice is: homicide, fraud, usury, inordinate anger, secret insinuation, and defamation. Our neighbor deserves his good name. When that is unjustly taken from him, public restitution is required.

Interior souls must be on guard not to give undue respect to others by taking from one and giving to another unjustly. The interior life can never be fruitful if one takes justice lightly.

Social justice bids us to render to society what we owe to it.[232] Equity is concerned with the spirit of the law and helps one avoid Pharisaism and to be wise and full of common sense. The rules of equity distribute social advantages and burdens, not according to favoritism but according to the capacity of each citizen.[233] Equity tends toward charity. An example includes helping starving prisoners of war.

How are justice and charity related? Justice means giving each one what is his due. Each one's due is a right. Charity means to love God above all and to love our neighbor as ourselves, which goes beyond merely giving each his due.

What virtues are related to Christian justice? Religion means to render God His due. Piety means to give honor to God, country, legitimate authority, and parents. This includes veracity in speech, respect, amiability, and liberality.[234]

The virtue of justice frees the soul from a false notion of independence by awakening it to the glory of God and the good of neighbor. This false notion often results in a bitter zeal that rashly judges, insinuates, and slanders neighbor and is often the source of secret egoism. To overcome this tendency, ask God for an infused justice, which Saint Thomas says "consists in the soul giving a whole-hearted consent to follow the way proposed."[235] The ways proposed are found in the Ten Commandments.

Why are patience and meekness needed to progress through the illuminative way? Some souls are by nature outgoing, and

---

[232] Tanquerey, Very Rev. Adolphe, *The Spiritual Life*, no. 1039.

[233] Tanquerey, Very Rev. Adolphe, *The Spiritual Life*, no. 1039.

[234] Liberality with resources is opposed to avarice and prodigality (altruism).

[235] *Summa Theologica* I–II, q. 61, a. 5.

some introverted. But they are each climbing the summit of the mountain by different paths. The outgoing person must ask for meekness, and the introverted person must ask for fortitude and patience.

Patience, illumined by faith, is a part of fortitude. Saint Thomas says patience "hinders a man from departing from right reason, by yielding to difficulties and sadness."[236] Asking God for this virtue sincerely will make an impatient man change into a patient man. Those who bear adversity through pride only have a counterfeit patience, or rather a hardness of heart. "The patient man is better than the valiant."[237] Patience makes us eager to embrace suffering in union with Jesus Christ and in order to make us more like that Divine Model.[238]

Longanimity resembles patience, but is special, likened to having a severe boss, because it involves a long trial for months or years. This virtue, when formed, helps us to resemble Christ, who was patient in His sufferings—that is why His suffering is called the Passion. God really shows His love when souls must suffer because of good people, friends, family, or coworkers in the vineyard. Christian patience is not stoic but reminds us to visit the Holy Face on the cross, recalling how He endured the ignominy for three hours. Remember, the saints remark that all sufferings endured with patience build our spiritual edifice, greatly ensuring our salvation.

What is the importance of meekness and its spiritual fruits? Meekness or gentleness means curbing the inordinate

---

[236] *Summa Theologica* II–II, q. 136, a. 1.

[237] Prov. 16:32.

[238] Tanquerey, Very Rev. Adolphe, *The Spiritual Life*, no. 1090.

movements of anger.[239] The soul who possesses it overcomes bitterness by calmness. Meekness is the flower of charity and is the lot of the saints. Just as the flower attracts the observer, souls corrected with gentleness are more likely to conform than if corrected with a just severity. Many souls are well intentioned, but their exterior roughness loses souls, for they seem to speak from passion rather than reason. "When faced with those who make us suffer, meekness helps one rejoice in these miseries and tribulations, well knowing that to suffer with Christ means to comfort Him."[240] A prime example is the flower of Saint Stephen, who, by meekness, prayed for the conversion of those who stoned him. Saint Augustine is said to have remarked, "If it were not for the prayers of St. Stephen, we would not have a St. Paul."

Like a broken reed reviving after some time of silence and waiting, a person who answers an accuser, not with like tone but with meekness, will also gradually recover and be stronger.

The gift of piety is related to meekness because it renders a filial affection toward God and allows one to see Him more as a very loving Father. It seems the souls of today suffer much from a bad perception of God our Father due to contemporary ills, divorce, alcoholism, and so on that bring about bad fathers, but the Holy Ghost, if asked sincerely for the gift of piety, can repair this relationship. Piety also helps souls overcome inordinate competition, for it helps to see brothers not as rivals but as children of our common Father.[241] Indeed, meekness, united to this gift of the Holy Ghost, is like the flower of charity.

---

[239] *Summa Theologica* II–II, q. 157, a. 1 f.

[240] Tanquerey, Very Rev. Adolphe, *The Spiritual Life*, no. 1090.

[241] *Summa Theologica* II–II, q. 122, a. 2.

If one wants to truly live the prelude of eternal life in the soul, he ought to ask for piety, meekness, and patience while looking on the Crucified, which is the highest expression of goodness on earth. Remember, at His baptism, Jesus was visited by a dove, a symbol of the Holy Ghost and sign of meekness. O Sacred Heart of Jesus, make my heart more like unto Thine!

## Why Is Chastity Required for Spiritual Fruitfulness?

Saint Thomas remarks that modesty is not a virtue but a natural good disposition; however, chastity is a Christian virtue. Chastity is an acquired virtue when *reason* calms the senses when they are occasionally troubled or heightened toward the flesh. Chasity is infused at Baptism and causes the light of *grace* when the senses are stirred. Virginity is higher because it offers to God lifelong continence. This requires one to watch and pray, to mortify the senses, and to avoid idleness.[242] Virginity gives the Church a certain splendor when women take on the habit and make a vow of virginity. This is also seen in the priesthood. The Flathead[243] Native Americans only sought Father De Smet, nicknamed "Blackrobe," to teach the tribe rather than married missionaries from Protestant sects.

Lack of chastity leads to many sorrows, like children out of wedlock, divorce, and its related family dishonor. The divorce of King Henry VIII led to a whole nation's schism and eventual heresy.

---

[242] Tanquerey, Very Rev. Adolphe, *The Spiritual Life*, no. 370.

[243] These Native Americans saw *blackrobes* in their dreams and knew they would teach the Christian faith to their tribe.

Chastity is lost by the senses, imagination, and the intention of the heart. The motive for chastity is love of God. That is mainly why a lack of chastity is sinful. If indulged, the sin of lust sprouts a hatred of God—because He is the one who commands chastity. Chastity is rightly called the angelic virtue because it likens us to the angels, who are by nature pure.[244] This lack of chastity is why the enkindling of the love of God has not taken place in our times as Jesus desired.

Maintaining chastity requires the soul to remain with the Crucified by a twofold mortification of the body and the heart. The rule is to refrain from excessive familiarity with the opposite sex and all exposure to occasions of sins against chastity, especially on the internet.

What are the fruits of chastity? St. John Climacus remarks: "He is truly virtuous upon whose spirit heavenly beauty is so engraved that he deigns not to cast a look upon earthly beauty, and thus feels no burning of the fire which consumes the hearts of other men."[245] Chastity makes the body become simple, like the gaze of the face of a saint in prayer. Saint Padre Pio's smile was attractive to many, especially American soldiers.[246] By purity, the body grows beautiful. The face expresses much about the chastity of a person. Reciting the name of Mary breathes forth purity and makes us become like clay in her hands so she can form us into incorruptible creatures.[247] Just think of the incorruptible saints. The highest level of chastity leads to

---

[244] Tanquerey, Very Rev. Adolphe, *The Spiritual Life*, no. 1100.

[245] St. John Climacus, *Ladder of Paradise*, Degree XV, 7 quoted from Tanquerey, *The Spiritual Life*, no. 1124.

[246] See Frank Rega, *Padre Pio and America*. During World War II, American soldiers frequently visited the saint in Pietrelcina, Italy.

[247] Tanquerey, Very Rev. Adolphe, *The Spiritual Life*, no. 1126.

spiritual marriage with God. Intimacy of Jesus and the soul is so complete that there is a perfect communion of ideas—sentiments, sacrifice, and salvation of souls, to name a few.

Perfect purity allows a soul to share in the spiritual paternity of God and the salvation of souls. Think of Saint Francis Xavier, who baptized millions. Purity prepares a soul to receive contemplation. This lack of virtue is why so few progress in the interior life today. By perfect purity, souls begin to see how God provides, and they see God in other souls.

Now, turn to the prayers to be recited during the *illuminative* way and the Chaplet of the Holy Face (p. 85, 20).

## Day 15

### The Holy Face on Tabor

It is a mystery why Jesus chose His most beloved, Peter, James, and John, to follow Him up to Mount Tabor. Was it because of their generosity, mortification, or humility? And why were Moses and Elias chosen to be present at the epiphany of the Face of Jesus, when It became dazzling as the sun and His raiment white as the snow? Moses was not worthy to enter the Promised Land because his faith was weak when he struck the rock twice before water flowed out. But in God's providence, he was given this wonderful blessing. Elias was also there, the great father of the mystical way.

God chose a place apart, for He does not converse with us in the midst of the world: "In order to hear him, the soul must be closed to the tumult of the world."[248] Elijah heard God on

[248] Fourault, *The Month of the Holy Face*, p. 145.

the mountain, not in the thunder or wind, but in the quiet whisper of God. Behold, in the New Testament, Jesus reveals the ray of glory of His Holy Face also on a mountain, a quiet place away from the world.

Behold, this beautiful Face, which constantly ravishes the angels, prompted Saint Peter to desire to remain and build dwelling tents. But as soon as the ray of consolation was unveiled, His Holy Face immediately assumed an expression of sorrow. When conversing with the greatest Prophets of the Law, He speaks of the excessive sufferings that He will endure at the hands of the high priest and his priest counselors, the scribes and the Pharisees. Peter is denied his desire to build tents in order to give us a lesson. Joys are so fleeting in this world. Suffering is the common lot for all, and the funeral veil of trial will not be lifted from our faces until the last day.[249] For we are simply wayfarers, and we are not permitted to fix our tent here.

As we have seen in the purgative way, God raises the soul to the mountain of consolation, but it is in the illuminative way, where so few dare to tread, that He reveals the royal road of suffering that leads to the path of the unitive way.

O divine Majesty, Jesus Christ, place in me the desire of lofty prayer and draw me to the mountain, like Saint Elijah, who discovered Thy voice in the silence there. In this calm, speak to my heart of the humility I must render toward Thee and neighbor. As Thy Passion was placed in my soul like a seed at Baptism, water it with Thy grace so that I may grow in Thy humility and magnanimity.

---

[249] Fourault, p. 148.

## The Humility of Proficients

What humility is required in proficients? Humility must be deeper than the humility in the soul in the purgative way because the excavation of a building must be deeper in proportion as the building is to be higher. Thus, the higher one advances in prayer, the greater the excavation needed to generate humility of soul, for a tall building without a sufficient excavation will eventually fall.

Why is humility necessary? It makes the proficient cling to God alone. No matter how much he sees others acting inordinately in word or deed, he himself will not depart from his uprightness of conduct.[250] "The entrance to paradise is not only narrow but low."[251]

What is humility toward God? Jesus told Saint Catherine of Siena a reality that would help her abandon herself to His will. "I am Who am. And thou are who are not."[252] This means bowing our face to the ground. It means recognizing the extreme poverty of soul. Those who have not committed mortal sin have innocence, but humility attributes that rare state due to the grace of God. Those who have committed mortal sin recognize their wretchedness through humility. It recognizes the infinite distance between Creator and creature. The higher one ascends in the interior life, which is union with God, the more humble he ought to be. We were made out of nothing. It is due to grace that we continue to exist. The humble soul is like the root of the spikenard. Spikenard is hidden in the ground, but it is the most useful of the herbs. Humility leads Christians to

---

250 *ST* II–II, q. 33, a. 5.

251 Bergamo, Fr. Gaetano Maria, *Humility of Heart*, p. 161.

252 Forbes, *St. Catherine of Siena*, p. 64.

desire the hidden place or last place, like Saint Paul, who considered himself the least of apostles because he persecuted the Church and Jesus. Christ showed us an example of humility when He was preferred to Barabbas, a murderer, for crucifixion.

Our Lady, who is most humble, needs to be our constant intercessor, for she will help us persevere in humility to the end: "pray for us now and at the hour of death." "The humble man," says St. Thomas, "is amazed when anyone speaks well of him and there is nothing that astonishes him more than to hear himself praised. The Blessed Virgin, when she heard from the Archangel Gabriel that she was to become the Mother of God had such a low opinion of herself that she marveled greatly that she should be exalted to such an eminent dignity."[253] Humility helps us from pusillanimity, "which is born of human respect or of spiritual sloth!"[254] Humility helps the soul tend to great things humbly.

What should humility be toward neighbors? Consider all others greater than oneself on account of their hidden virtues. Remember, if we do not commit sin, it is because God gives us the movement of goodness. The only thing we can claim is sin. Humility does not flee great things. That is pusillanimity, which refuses the necessary toil for great things. Humility also opposes human respect, which refuses to do right out of the fear of the wrath of wicked men. The more humble a soul is, the stronger he is. The humble man does not take pleasure in praise but gives the glory to God. "Not to us, O Lord, not to us, but to thy name be given the glory."[255] The humble soul patiently endures

---

[253] Bergamo, Fr. Gaetano Maria, *Humility of Heart*, p. 181.
[254] Garrigou-Lagrange, p. 122.
[255] Ps. 113:9.

deserved reproaches. The humble soul prefers suffering. Father Olier says the humility of proficients is wanting to be known as vile, as base, as being nothing but sin, and to be considered as such by all men.[256]

What was the humility and magnanimity of Christ? Saint Paul captured it well, "He humbled Himself, becoming obedient unto death."[257] Humility is obedient, pride does its own will. Humility renders fruitful what seems most useless: suffering. Christ was born in the cold of a stable; thus He showed us suffering at the first moment of His appearance to the world. Saint Leo summed it up, "Humility is sustained by majesty, weakness by power, mortality by eternity. If the Savior were not truly God, He would not bring the remedy; and if He were not truly man, He would not be an example for us."[258] God desired the first adorers to be shepherds.[259] "The two extremes are united: The Word was made flesh."[260]

What is the unity of humility and Christian dignity? On one hand, the saints proclaimed their wretchedness, and on the other, they had a superhuman dignity. Saint Catherine took care of lepers in the hospital despite the mockery she received because she saw Christ on their faces. God sometimes permits some infirmity so that we may understand our relationship with Him. We cannot persevere with our own strength. Saint Paul was favored by many supernatural communications, but

---

[256] Tanquerey, Very Rev. Adolphe, *The Spiritual Life*, no. 1134.

[257] Phil. 2:8.

[258] Leo the Great, *Sermo 1 de Nativitate Domini*. Office of Matins for Christmas.

[259] See Ps. 81.

[260] Leo the Great, *Sermo 1 de Nativitate Domini*. Office of Matins for Christmas.

God visited him with a sting in the flesh to keep him humble. Divine power is shown in weakness. This is why it is a good habit to constantly tell God of our weakness. "Humility empties the soul of self-love and vain-glory, and thus creates there a vast capacity for grace, which God is ready to fill, for as St. Bernard says there is a close affinity between grace and humility: 'The virtue of humility is always found closely associated with Divine grace.'"[261]

Now, turn to the prayers to be recited during the *illuminative* way and the Chaplet of the Holy Face (p. 85, 20).

## Day 16

### The Holy Face Weeps over Jerusalem

At the sight of Jerusalem, Jesus grieves and sheds tears on the city of greatest benediction—the city of peace, Salem, the elected city of the Temple worship and the First Mass, the Last Supper. What passes through the mind of Jesus? Why does He weep so, the tears inundating His Face? He sees the triumphal entrance of the Hebrews into the promised land, the Temple receiving the cloud of God's presence, the songs of David and of Solomon chanted and accompanied by harp in the Temple, the crowds of people swelling into the millions during the Paschal ceremonies.

On the other side, He sees the hardening of heart of the Pharisees and scribes, the ones who were chosen to lead the assembly to God but chose to sentence Jesus to death. His

[261] Tanquerey, Very Rev. Adolphe, *The Spiritual Life*, no. 1137, quoting St. Bernard, *Super Missu Est*, Homil. IV, 9.

divine eyes foresee the destruction of the Temple, and when He looks to the west, He sees on the mountain a cross and traces of blood. His gaze moves from the Jerusalem to our souls.

Why does He weep over our souls? Our souls are given every help from the Face of Jesus, but we constantly betray His look. "For the just man shall fall seven times and shall rise again."[262] "Behold, O God our protector: and look on the face of thy Christ."[263]

May Thy tears, O Jesus, stream down Thy furrowed cheeks as Thou weep over Jerusalem and help me to become obedient to the inspirations of the Holy Ghost. By Thy tears, bestow Thy grace upon me to live the spirit of poverty as Thine example. Lastly, present Thy tears to the Father on my behalf for the spirit of simplicity and veracity, that I may merit the higher levels of contemplation and the rewards of eternal life.

## The Spirit of Poverty, Obedience, and Simplicity

God bestows His favors on the little ones like the rain, a symbol of grace, which falls on the mountaintops and flows into the valleys. Thus, the grace of God falls on the proud who reject it, and it flows to the little ones who live in the valley of poverty, obedience, and simplicity.

Why is voluntary poverty valued? Perfection can be reached if the soul has at least the spirit of the counsels of poverty, chastity, and obedience. Jesus surrounds Himself with Apostles, ignorant and uncouth, and therefore little esteemed,

---

262 Prov. 24:16.

263 Ps. 83:10.

eleven fishermen and a publican. He shows a marked preference for those whom the world despises, the poor, sinners, the afflicted, little children, those disowned by the world.[264] Poverty can be lived in a detached abundance of worldly goods or in destitution out of the love of God. Poverty allows us to possess God when we give Him to others, because spiritual goods are infinitely abundant when given to others. Material goods are limited; thus, the spirit of poverty, or detachment, helps interior souls to understand the importance of private property by not infringing on the rights of others and by giving to those who are in need.[265] The spirit of poverty, in this line of thought, allows one who takes bread out of absolute necessity, with the intention to repay its owner when possible, not to be guilty of theft.

The spirit of poverty helps one to avoid the excesses of capitalism and communism. The sin of the capitalist is making money his god and not giving to those in need. The sin of the communist is seeing the state as god.

Poverty is a counsel and is not obligatory. Some practice poverty of heart by retaining their capital but use the income only according to the wise spiritual director, and thus they remain in a state in which God's providence has placed them, they live in the practice of detachment of mind and heart.[266] For example, Saint Louis, king of France, was not poor, yet he had three poor people dine with him almost every day.

What is the fruitfulness of poverty? Saint Thomas lists four points. It:

---

[264] Tanquerey, Very Rev. Adolphe, *The Spiritual Life*, no. 1142.
[265] Cf. 1 Tim. 6:17–19.
[266] Tanquerey, Very Rev. Adolphe, *The Spiritual Life*, no. 899.

1. fructifies preaching (e.g., Franciscans who live lady poverty have a certain gift from God to preach.),
2. augments the salvation of souls,
3. helps one focus on eternal goods, and
4. gives grace in the absence of human helps.[267]

Jesus chose poor fisherman to show the world that it was God working through uneducated men.

What is the fruitfulness of total slavery to the Blessed Virgin Mary? She is a treasury that will not let our merits spoil. Souls who give all their property in a total consecration receive more than a hundredfold for their donation. This sacrifice allows Mary to allocate all goods of her slaves with her wisdom as the Mother of God. Her clients become proficient at giving God the glory that is His due and obtaining the salvation of souls.

What is the grandeur of obedience? "Obedience is the mother and guardian of the other virtues, and transforms our ordinary actions into so many virtuous acts."[268] Pride turns us directly away from God, but other sins turn us less directly from God.[269] Obedience delivers us from self-will. Saint Bernard says, "Take away self-will, and there will no longer be any hell."[270] Fasts and penances done out of pride are rejected by God. Pride renders honor to our *way* of doing good *instead* of doing the good itself.

---

[267] *Summa Theologica* III, q. 40, a. 3; q. 35 at. 7.

[268] Tanquerey, Very Rev. Adolphe, *The Spiritual Life*, no. 1067.

[269] *Summa Theologica* I–II, q. 73, a. 5. "Spiritual sins are of greater guilt than carnal sins."

[270] Garrigou-Lagrange, *The Three Ages of the Interior Life*, vol. 2, p. 151.

The vow of obedience must be practiced in the spirit of faith, which allows one to see God's Providence[271] in a superior despite his defects. Obedience is one that comes hardest to human nature because we are attached to our own will. To overcome criticism of authority figures, we need to see God's Providence operating in our superiors. True obedience is the best proof of love, to practice it is to grow in the virtue of charity.[272]

What are the fruits of obedience? Saint Thomas says that it is more perfect to offer God one's will and judgment than to offer Him exterior goods through voluntary poverty or one's body through chastity.[273]

These are the chief three fruits:

1. Great rectitude of judgment, because obedience makes us participate in the very wisdom of God seeing all as God sees all.
2. Great strength of the will, without going so far as martyrdom. Obedience works prodigies. Sr. Marie de St. Pierre was told by her superiors to write her autobiography. Saint Thérèse of the Little Child and of the Holy Face read it under obedience and, through reading it, numbered it as one of the causes of her most popular "Little Way" and particular holiness.
3. The highest liberty of spirit, because it makes us true children of God, which brings with it a singular intimacy with Him. It places oneself like a docile instru-

---

[271] This is a key distinction in obedience—the superior is not God, but is an instrument of Divine Providence.

[272] Tanquerey, Very Rev. Adolphe, *The Spiritual Life*, no. 371.

[273] *Summa Theologica* II–II, q. 104, a. 3 c et ad 1una.

> ment in the hands of God. "Obedience delivers us from doubts, hesitations, and anxieties. It simplifies life while elevating it." It prepares us for a loftier contemplation of divine things.[274]

What is simplicity and uprightness? "Be ye therefore wise as serpents and simple as doves."[275] Saint Thérèse of the Child Jesus and of the Holy Face captures it well: "Far from resembling those beautiful souls who, from their childhood, practiced all sorts of lacerations, I made mine consist solely in breaking my will, in withholding an answer, in rendering little services without drawing attention to them and many other things of this kind. . . . One has only to love Him, without looking at oneself, without too greatly examining one's defects. *A glance toward Jesus and the knowledge of one's own wretchedness make reparation for everything.*"[276]

The simple and upright soul judges everything according to the divine light and wills only what God wills. Notice the simplicity of Jesus. He answers Pilate simply when asked if He was a king. "My kingdom is not of this world."[277] Some of the saints who were illiterate were prodigies. They had a profound understanding of divine things. When Saint Joan of Arc was asked if she was in the state of grace, she said that if she was, she prayed that God keep her there, and if she was not, that God bring her there. Simple souls who have discretion fare well in persecution because they are reminded that no matter what

---

[274] Garrigou-Lagrange, *The Three Ages of the Interior Life*, vol. 2, p. 157.

[275] Matt. 10:16.

[276] *L'Espirit de sainte Thérèse de l'Enfant-Jésui*, pp. 163–86.

[277] John 18:36.

happens "to them that love God [and persevere in this love], all things work together unto good."[278]

Veracity goes with simplicity. Veracity is part of justice because men owe each other the truth. Not every truth needs to be revealed, but when speaking, truth must be said because it is good and worthy of praise.[279] Veracity is indispensable to the life of society. When society collapses and indiscrete questions or violence to human rights arise, secrets can still be kept to protect the innocent without offending the truth. To this end, a true Christian is habitually listening to the inspirations from above. He who wishes to progress through the illuminative way, thus deepening in the interior life, inclines him to keep silent about his own qualities.[280] Habitually remaining in the truth inclines us to devotion and spiritual joy.[281]

What are defects opposed to simplicity? Perfidy inclines a man to be disloyal to what should command his loyalty. Duplicity is deliberate and inspires lies, simulation, and hypocrisy. Boasting occurs because one talks about himself in a manner that artificially elevates-what he really is.[282]

Some have said that to reject the known truth is the sin against the Holy Ghost. Why? Our intellects were made for truth and simplicity, but remaining in a state where a soul knows it is living a lie cuts off all divine inspiration. This quality is especially dangerous when found in priests and religious.

Now, turn to the prayers to be recited during the *illuminative* way and the Chaplet of the Holy Face (p. 85, 20).

---

[278] Rom. 8:28.

[279] *ST* II–II, q. 110, a. 3.

[280] *Summa Theologica* II–II, q. 109, a. 4.

[281] *ST* II–II, q. 82, a. 4.

[282] *ST* II–II, q. 112, a. 1.

# Day 17

## The Holy Face in the Agony

Jesus turns His Holy Face from Jerusalem and enters the grotto. Notice the train of angels there to assist Him. He bows down His Face to the ground.

Why has Jesus chosen this place for His agony? Perhaps because, according to ancient tradition, this is where our first parents took refuge after expulsion from the Garden of Eden, even as Golgotha was the place of Adam's burial.

Why does He place His Holy Face on the ground, weeping and sweating blood? He sees all our sins in all their hideousness. His eyes cannot bear the sight.

Contemplate His pale Face drenched in a cold sweat. Jesus has agreed to do as His Father wills, and He has put His Sacred Heart in the wine press of love. The blood sweats out of his pores and flows to the ground as it will at the Scourging and the Crucifixion. It saturates His hair and beard.

Behold the choir of angels assigned from all eternity the privilege to assist our Holy Redeemer during this profound mystery. Jesus teaches us to suffer, to suffer with Him, to grow in the spirit of faith, with confidence in His Father and abandonment to His divine plan. Just as the humanity of Jesus called upon the help of the angels, we too must have peace about our future agonies because we will have more than consoling angels: Jesus will be our chief consoler.

"My Father, if it be possible, let this chalice pass from me. Nevertheless not as I will, but as thou wilt."[283] "Incorporated into Christ, those in the agony of suffering await with invincible trust that Heaven where Jesus has prepared a home for them

---

[283] Matt. 26:39.

and where they already abide, through hope, in the Person of their Saviour. 'For we are saved by hope.'"[284]

## The Spirit of Faith, Hope in God, Love of Abandonment in God

Man lives either according to nature or faith. The spirit of faith is the manner of judging things from a higher point of view. Living by nature alone is spiritual blindness, and one does not internally grow in divine things.

Faith is a gift from God. One should constantly ask for it and for its increase. It is a spiritual sense enabling us to penetrate the revealed mysteries before we are admitted to see God Face to face. Notice when some say, "God's ways are too deep." Faith must be asked for; thus God will freely give the spiritual sense to see deeper and according to His ways. When God infuses faith, the soul participates in eternal life before being admitted to heaven. Saint Francis de Sales[285] says that God enters our soul and speaks to us by inspiration (not by way of discourse).

How does one grow in infused faith? Remember, in the interior life, the soul must always be progressing; thus, faith should daily increase in us. Jesus knew the souls of His disciples, that they were slow and "of little faith,"[286] whereas He said to the woman at Canaan, "O woman great is thy faith."[287] The

---

[284] Tanquerey, Very Rev. Adolphe, *The Spiritual Life*, no. 1203, quoting Rom. viii, 24.

[285] Francis de Sales, *Treatise on Love of God*, Bk. II, ch. 4.

[286] Matt. 6:30.

[287] Matt. 15:28.

Canaanite woman possessed what the disciples lacked: internal generosity and docility, two qualities that God loves to reward with an increase in faith.

Why is Faith necessary? It is the foundation of our supernatural life. It strengthens the soul and unites it to God.[288] It is the light which illumines our intellect and differentiates the Christian from the philosopher.[289]

What are some practical points to help one grow in faith? We should consider God in the light of faith, not by our own opinion. If we listen to ourselves and ascribe to the Lord our own reflections, they are more or less inspired by our self-love. God does not visit a soul in self-love; rather, He visits a soul steeped in the mysteries of His life and death. Baptism gives one the light of these mysteries, and these graces grow with fervent Communions.

True faith helps us to discover our defects and predominant faults, the obstacles that hinder us in holiness. When perceiving one's neighbor, take care to renounce pettiness, pride, or jealousies. See superiors as representatives of God. Look at all the events of life in the light of faith, even apparent contradictions. See purifications as well merited punishment for hidden sins for which no one reproves us. Saint John Eudes knew that if God visits us with chronic sufferings, it shows how much He loves us, because the pain of purgatory would be one thousand times worse and without merit.

What does confidence or hope in God look like for proficients? Hope in God cannot be weak and intermittent, but it must be firm, humble, and persevering. Ask for that.

---

[288] Tanquerey, Very Rev. Adolphe, *The Spiritual Life*, no. 1172.

[289] Tanquerey, Very Rev. Adolphe, *The Spiritual Life*, no. 1176.

Hope is not presumption or its opposite, despair. Presumption means not asking God enough for His help. It also means expecting God to grant things that He cannot grant, like eternal life without effort.[290] Presumption easily makes one oscillate to despair because the work of sanctification is too difficult. That is why hope is symbolized by an anchor, which does not oscillate.

What is hope? Hope is not born of our own effort, but given by God when we desire God for Himself. Desiring merely to make it to heaven is not living the virtue of hope. Hope gives us the courage to suffer what it takes to not settle for an inferior degree in heaven. Heaven is our true country, true happiness, true destiny.[291]

How do we know we are going to heaven? No man can be certain of salvation without a special revelation, which is rare; thus, we should not presume. Some of the saints received this gift, but their destiny was verified. Hope is the expectation of a good difficult to obtain; namely, God through His assisting omnipotence.[292] If one takes a plane to Boston, he is not absolutely certain of his arrival there but can count on the likelihood of going in the right direction. Thus, we tend certainly toward salvation through faith according to the promises of God.

What are some qualities of hope? "He that shall persevere unto the end, he shall be saved."[293] Hope keeps us from presumption. Presumption consists in expecting from God Heaven and the graces necessary to reach it, without willing to

---

[290] It is a modern error to think the only thing required to get to heaven is death.

[291] Tanquerey, Very Rev. Adolphe, *The Spiritual Life*, no. 1202.

[292] Tanquerey, Very Rev. Adolphe, *The Spiritual Life*, no. 1193.

[293] Matt. 10:22.

take the means He has ordained.[294] When God communicates hope, it should be firm and invincible. Hope should not be broken by trials, but rather, trials should purify and work for our salvation. Hope should not let us get focus on the past or future, because we can do nothing about either. Saint Catherine used to say: "Never consider your past sins except in the light of infinite mercy." But keep in mind, these are past confessed sins.

Saint Thérèse of the Child Jesus and of the Holy Face summed it up: hope is not on us but on God. Her immense confidence in God came from her ardent love of Jesus dwelling in her soul. "Yet I know my Jesus, that you never command the impossible; You know better than I do how frail and imperfect I am; You know perfectly well that I can never hope to love my Sisters as You love them, unless You Yourself love them in me."[295]

What are the fruits of hope? A sign is that we take pleasure not only in future glory but also in our trials and tribulation. Trial causes hope to grow. Saint Philip Neri used to pray: "I thank Thee with my whole heart, Lord God, that things do not go as I should like them to, but as Thou dost wish. It is better that they should go according to Thy way, which is better than mine." Lastly, although we may not *feel* hope in God, we should make *acts* of hope in God.

How does a proficient love the will of God? A sign of imperfect love means one serves God for his own interests. But charity is a love of friendship we should have for God because

---

[294] Tanquerey, Very Rev. Adolphe, *The Spiritual Life*, no. 1201.

[295] St. Thérèse, of the Child Jesus and of the Holy Face, *The Story of a Soul*, p. 126.

He is good. Proficients "who have already made some progress are sustained by the hope and desire of heavenly things, and though they do not seek the Cross, they willingly carry it with a certain joy, knowing that each new pang represents an additional degree of glory."[296]

If a soul loves in this way, with final perseverance, he will be able to delight in this love beyond his imagination.

What is the measure of love of God? In a word, it is to love what God loves. It is not the first degree of love, which is loving God in prosperity. It is not the second degree of loving the divine will and the commandments. But it is in the highest degree, to love God in tribulation and sufferings. Saint Charles, archbishop of Milan, took to such poverty "that he was (in his episcopal palace) like a dog in the house of its master." He chose to love God in tribulation and sufferings.

The love of conformity to the divine will is like a fire. The most arid wood burns hottest. Meditation on the Passion roots our love in solid rock. Abandonment to God's will, daily and hourly, are the baby steps to a great love. Our love of God grows by carrying our cross. "Thereby the soul acquires one by one all the virtues of Our Lord."[297] It makes the soul rejoice at everything that contributes to the glory of God.

Now, turn to the prayers to be recited during the *illuminative* way and the Chaplet of the Holy Face (p. 85, 20).

---

[296] Tanquerey, Very Rev. Adolphe, *The Spiritual Life*, no. 429.

[297] Tanquerey, Very Rev. Adolphe, *The Spiritual Life*, no. 497.

## Day 18

### The Kiss of the Traitor on the Holy Face of Jesus

Sweet Holy Face of Jesus, rising from prayer and knowing in Thy heart the traitor Judas is approaching. What does Thy Face reflect in this agony, this deed of treachery as it comes? Does it show us an expression of sadness? When we commit sin, does it also bring sadness to Thy adorable Face?

Behold, Judas approaches with a train of armed guards. At the Last Supper, Thou did just share the Bread of Life, the pledge of immortality, the Holy Sacrament of the Altar. But Judas made the first sacrilegious Communion.

Judas approaches Jesus in the dark, while Jesus softly says, "Friend whereto art thou come?"[298] Judas embraces Jesus and places a kiss on His Holy Face. Why does Jesus call him "friend"? "Though you may love me no longer, I love you always, and my heart remains still open to you, in spite of the shame which covers my face."[299]

What treachery! Judas was allowed intimate conversation with the Redeemer; he was allowed to perform miracles; the Blessed Virgin Mary was ever so tender to him by her words, and she constantly prayed that he would not be sifted by the devil. He received the Word of the promise of the happiness of eternal life, but he sold Christ for thirty pieces of silver.

At least, oh Lord, never allow me to receive a sacrilegious Communion and leave Mass early without giving the proper thanksgiving for at least ten minutes. Grant me the grace to

---

[298] Matt. 26:50.

[299] Fourault, *The Month of the Holy Face*, p. 178.

overcome my sins and become an apostle of Thy Holy Face by making reparation for the outrages I have inflicted upon Thee. May my life from henceforward be one of constant prayer for Thy glory and the salvation of souls so that when I appear at the particular judgment, Thou will call me friend. Give me the kiss of a happy judgment so that I may enter eternal life to contemplate Thee Face to face.

## Fraternal Charity and Zeal for the Glory of God and Salvation of Souls

Why should our love for God extend to our neighbor? Our Lord demands it. Natural love inclines us to do good to please others. But this leads us to love the kind and hate those who do evil. But Christ calls us to a supernatural love, "Love your enemies: do good to them who hate you: and pray for them that persecute and calumniate you."[300]

Jesus came to overthrow paganism and plant the Kingdom of God. "This commandment is new," says Bossuet, "Because Jesus Christ adds to the old this important feature of loving one another as *He has loved us*."[301] What is a good test to see if we truly have love for God? If we do not love our neighbor, our love of God is a lie.

Father Garrigou-Lagrange relates a beautiful story of love and its subsequent increase of faith:

> A young Jew whom we knew, the son of a Vienna banker, one day had the opportunity to take vengeance on his

[300] Matt. 5:44.

[301] Tanquerey, Very Rev. Adolphe, *The Spiritual Life*, no. 1246, quoting *Meditations, La Cène,* I Part. 75e jour.

> family's greatest enemy; as he was about to do so, he remembered the following words of Scripture, which he was in the habit of reading from time to time: "Forgive us our trespasses, as we forgive those who trespass against us." Then, instead of taking vengeance, he fully pardoned his enemy and immediately received the grace of faith. He believed in the entire Gospel, and a short time afterward entered the Church and became a priest and religious. The precept of fraternal charity had illumined him.[302]

What is the effect of charity? Charity disposes us to judge well of our neighbor and to supply them with their wishes, save going against the commandments. Through fraternal charity, painful things we impose on ourselves for our neighbor are fruitful. Fraternal charity preserves us from clashing with our neighbor and helps us to make reconciliation as soon as possible. There is a radiating goodness of those who strive for this charity, as God gives recipients the union of hearts with God.

How far should fraternal charity extend? It should be universal and without limit. It is much different in hell, for those inhabitants no longer desire to rise from their hatred. As charity grows in a soul, it recognizes the need to give greater esteem to those nearer to God in sanctity. Thus, jealousies go away.

How does one make progress in fraternal charity? Through adversity. The devil works hard sowing vice in holy monasteries but sleeps at the gate of wicked cities. Why? In God's providence, He permits temptations on proficient souls so that through adversity, they may receive an increase of virtue. Mother Mariana led such an admirable life of heroic fraternal charity that she accepted the challenge of Jesus to suffer

---

[302] Garrigou-Lagrange, p. 202.

the pains of hell for five years in order to save one of the nuns from hell who was captain of the non-observant nuns in Quito, Ecuador.[303]

Through prayer, ask God to give an understanding of temperament clashes. What does this mean? Our neighbor may not be sinning when causing clashes with us, but it may simply be a defect in temperament. Sometimes, the most saintly souls are the most "trying" to us. Remember that God loves them, so we must love them. The benevolent view helps us to overcome rash judgment. "Judge not, that you may not be judged. For with what judgment you judge, you shall be judged, and with what measure you mete, it shall be measured to you again."[304]

What are the descriptions of rash judgment?

1. It is a judgment. It consists in affirming evil on a slight indication.
2. It is often false. How do we know the inner thoughts or the prayer to God of our neighbor?
3. It is likely a sin against charity because even if we are right, we arrogate that jurisdiction to ourselves when it belongs to God alone. The weeds of rash judgment are malevolence, often expressed with the mask of benevolence, which is only a grimace against charity. God usually visits the guilty here by withdrawing one from contemplation of divine things: it becomes, as it were, a veil over the eyes of the spirit.

[303] See *The Admirable Life of Mother Mariana*, Vol. I and II.
[304] Matt. 7:1–2.

How does one overcome rash judgment? We bear our neighbor's defects, return good for evil, avoid jealousy, and pray for the union of hearts.

Jealousy is easily overcome if we see our neighbor with the eyes of faith. We benefit by the merits of others, so we rejoice in the good qualities of others. Inferiors are weaker, usually, and superiors have a greater burden.

What does zeal for the glory of God and salvation of souls look like? Charity motivates a certain ardor of the glory of God, the imitation of the Lord, the salvation of souls, and the relief of souls in purgatory. Forbes captures well the zeal in St. Catherine of Siena: "We know from her own words that for the salvation of others she was ready to bear the pains of Hell. 'I am fain to offer Thee my body in sacrifice and to bear all for the world's sins that Thou mayest spare it, and exchange its life for another.'"[305]

The quality of zeal should be enduring ardor, not short-lived like the seed sown on rock. Zeal ought to be selfless, enlightened, patient, meek, and disinterested. "Zeal animated only by the natural spirit, instead of converting souls to God, gradually allows itself to be converted to the world." That is why many popular Catholic speakers, who are not rooted in virtue, leave the Church for the world. A remedy to this is to do our duties well in the state God has given us. Be faithful to prayer, the Mass, the Rosary, and particular devotions.

Should zeal be disinterested, avoiding appropriating to self what belongs to God? Yes, "Filled then, with esteem and admiration in God we long to have His Holy Name blessed, exalted, praised, honored, adored all over the earth."[306] Misplaced zeal is

---

[305] F. A. Forbes, *St. Catherine of Siena*, p. 12.

[306] Tanquerey, Very Rev. Adolphe, *The Spiritual Life*, no. 1231.

like the hunting dog that retrieves the bird and eats it for itself. The owner rightly gives it a severe beating. We should avoid the trap of doing good only the way we want.

In summary, zeal is humble and meek, snatches souls from hell, and likens our souls to the sweetness of the Blessed Virgin Mary and the saints. It imitates Our Lord.

How does one obtain zeal? This fire is something God wants to give every soul if they are constant in prayer. It should become continual so the soul is docile to every prompting of the Holy Ghost.

Now, turn to the prayers to be recited during the *illuminative* way and the Chaplet of the Holy Face (p. 85, 20).

# Day 19

## The Holy Face and Peter

Since Jesus, being God, is goodness itself, He wants what is good for us even more than we want our own good. Being God, He saw straight to the soul of Saint Peter. Jesus, looking upon Simon, said to him, "Thou art Simon son of John, henceforth thou shalt be called Cephas, that is to say stone."[307] "He turns His Holy Face towards a poor fisherman, and He discovers in him what no one had hitherto seen: an elect soul, a future fisher of men, he who was destined to be the cornerstone on which His Church was to be built."[308]

The eyes of Jesus and the radiance of His Holy Face so penetrated into the soul of Peter that he immediately left his nets, family, and land, and followed his benevolent master. This was

---

[307] John 1:42.

[308] Fourault, *The Month of the Holy Face*, p. 187.

Peter's first conversion, but he would need to endure two more before he would truly follow Jesus.

Before the fall of Saint Peter, he followed his Master with a mercenary love, a service not pure in intention, reflecting on what he might *get* out of the relationship. Thinking in this way, he said, "Although all shall be scandalized in thee, I will never be scandalized."[309] He was presumptuous and not discerning the spirit of mere nature. How often are we just like Peter, wanting of the second conversion?

The first pope denied Jesus three times to a maid while warming his hands outside of the mock trial of Jesus. Jesus forgets His own sufferings and ignominies, and thinking of raising up the first pope, "turning looked on Peter . . . and Peter going out wept bitterly."[310] "A ray of light and love, proceeding from the eyes of the Master, penetrates into the heart of the faithless disciple, and Peter confesses his fault."[311] It is said that he wept so bitterly that a rivulet of ceaseless tears traced upon Peter an indelible furrow marking his second conversion.

His contrition was so great that he was more fervent, as some theologians believe, after the fall than before. Where did he go? Did he confess his sin to the Blessed Virgin Mary, since the sacrament of confession was not promulgated, she who represented the future Church? Peter's third conversion into the unitive way would happen at Pentecost. He was then ready to suffer anything for his Master. As he was not worthy to do as his Master, he asked to be crucified upside down.

Dear Holy Spirit, visit me with a docile spirit, that I too may go through the three conversions like Saint Peter. Allow me

---

309 Matt. 26:33.

310 Luke 22:61–62.

311 Fourault, *The Month of the Holy Face*, pp. 189–90.

to be passive to Thee so Thou may blow like the wind into my soul, as sails of a ship, the seven gifts of Thy Holy Ghost. Draw me to Thyself ever more quickly so that I may contemplate the sweet Face of Jesus as He looked upon Saint Peter. Saint Peter, intercede for me so that I will overcome my imperfect intentions and serve God in His kingdom faithfully.

## Docility to the Holy Ghost and the Discerning of Spirits

The sevenfold gifts help us to receive the inspirations of the Holy Ghost with promptness and docility. They are infused and permanent habits.[312]

In the virtues, like religion, we more or less move ourselves, for example, to go to Mass. But by the gifts, we are more or less moved by a special inspiration of the Holy Ghost, for example, in the course of study, to pray in order to receive light. In virtues, we are more active, and in the gifts, we are more passive.

What are the seven Gifts of the Holy Ghost?[313]

1. Gift of Fear: The gift of fear inclines our will to filial respect for God, removes us from sin, which is displeasing to Him, and gives us hope in the power of His help. "Know you not," said Our Lord to St. Catherine of Sienna, "that all the sufferings a soul undergoes or could undergo in this life are not sufficient punishment for even the slightest fault?"[314]

---

[312] Unless mortal sin is committed.

[313] Enumerated according to the list of Isaias.

[314] Tanquerey, Very Rev. Adolphe, *The Spiritual Life*, no. 1335–1336,

2. Piety: is the begetting in our hearts of a filial affection for God and a tender devotion towards those persons and things consecrated to Him, in order to make us fulfil our religious duties with a holy joy.[315] Piety disposes the soul to the prayer of quiet.
3. Knowledge: is a gift which, by the illuminating action of the Holy Ghost, perfects the virtue of faith, and thereby gives us a knowledge of created things in their relation to God.[316] It helps us to weep for our sins.
4. Fortitude: is a *gift* which perfects the *virtue* of fortitude, by imparting to the will an impulse and an energy which enable it to do great things joyfully and fearlessly despite all obstacles.[317]
5. Counsel: perfects the virtue of prudence by making us judge promptly and rightly, as by a sort of supernatural intuition, what must be done, especially in difficult cases.[318]

---

quoting *Dialogue,* Bk. I, Ch. II. Also think of seeing the Holy Face of Jesus at the particular judgment. Will it be filial or servile fear?

[315] Tanquerey, Very Rev. Adolphe, *The Spiritual Life*, no. 1325. Think with the eyes of faith the Eucharistic Holy Face of Jesus and how He looks at the soul from the tabernacle.

[316] Tanquerey, Very Rev. Adolphe, *The Spiritual Life*, no. 1340. Think of the ray of light of Moses and the Holy Face of Jesus at Tabor and how it gives the light of faith to the soul.

[317] Tanquerey, Very Rev. Adolphe, *The Spiritual Life*, no. 1330. Think of the Face of Jesus after the Kiss of Judas. Did His Holy Face shine brightly when he said, "I am," when the soldiers fell backward to the ground?

[318] Tanquerey, Very Rev. Adolphe, *The Spiritual Life*, no. 1321. Think of the Holy Ghost at the Baptism of Jesus in the Jordan. What was the expression of the Holy Face toward the dove, symbol of counsel?

6. Understanding: is a gift which, under the enlightening action of the Holy Ghost, gives us a deep insight into revealed truths, without however giving a complete comprehension of the mysteries themselves.[319]
7. Wisdom: is a gift which perfects the virtue of charity by enabling us to discern God and divine things in their ultimate principles, and by giving us a relish for them.[320]

What conditions are required for docility to the Holy Ghost? Silence and having a constant conversation with God, instead of being preoccupied with the self, the devil, or the world, are first required. Docility helps us see clearly the nothingness of all the world's prizes; it helps us to penetrate the hidden harmony that exists between the soul and God. And it helps us to relish all things divine.[321]

What acts can we do to prepare for docility to the Holy Ghost? First, obey the will of God. Second, frequently renew our resolution to follow the will of God in everything. Third, ask for the light from the Holy Ghost to do the will of God. Fourth, make a consecration to the Holy Ghost.

Our age is wonderfully one of total consecrations to:

---

[319] Tanquerey, Very Rev. Adolphe, *The Spiritual Life*, no. 1344. Think of the Holy Face of Jesus and its reaction when the disciples understood a parable.

[320] Tanquerey, Very Rev. Adolphe, *The Spiritual Life*, no. 1349. Think of the Holy Face of Jesus when his apostles hand out the loaves and the fish on the Mount of Beatitudes.

[321] Tanquerey, Very Rev. Adolphe, *The Spiritual Life*, no. 1356.

1. the Sacred Heart of Jesus,
2. the Holy Ghost,
3. the Blessed Virgin Mary's Immaculate Heart,
4. Saint Joseph's Most Pure Heart, and
5. the Holy Face of Jesus. The first four lead souls in a mysterious way to the Holy Trinity, the Divinity. The Holy Face of Jesus is also a pathway to the Divinity. Thus, consecration to the Holy Face of Jesus is the fruit of true devotion to the preceding consecrations. Saint Joseph's and Mary's influence lead us to the humanity of Jesus, who leads us to the Holy Ghost, who introduces us to the mystery of the adorable Trinity. These consecrations are "a turning point in our spiritual life."[322]

What are the fruits of docility to the Holy Ghost? It is one thing to have exterior acts of virtue, but it is another, more perfect way to follow one's interior action, governed by the Holy Ghost, who ought to direct our powers and senses. The Holy Ghost is a Paraclete and Comforter and consoles us in our exile on earth while we are far from God. Saint John of the Cross speaks of this interior life of docility as a cellar. The last and inmost cellar, the spiritual marriage, is entered by few in this world.[323]

How does one discern the spirits? Elijah did not hear God in the whirlwind but in the gentle whisper. Interior silence and habitual recollection are required to hear the voice of God.

---

[322] Verheylezoon, Fr. S.J., *Devotion to the Sacred Heart*, p. 126.

[323] St. John of the Cross, *Spiritual Canticles*, Stanza 26, par. 2 f.

Discernment of spirits is extraordinary or ordinary. The subject at hand deals with ordinary discernment and is a wise discretion of those who faithfully practice prudence and the higher help of the gift of counsel. There are three different kinds of spirits that act on souls:

1. Devil: this spirit brings fear, anxiety, sophistries, subtleties, and illusions. “He resembles an artful lawyer defending a bad case;”
2. The world: this spirit makes us lazy, complain, lose patience, lose heart in the midst of trials and aridity. It can also be called the human spirit;
3. God: His spirit is good and gives us peace because God is the author of peace. He alone can penetrate into the inmost recesses of the soul and draw it to Himself.[324]

The world and the devil constantly interfere with souls; thus, a soul cannot be judged by one or two incidents but by his whole life. One can tell what spirit reigns in the soul by determining whether there is good or bad fruit.

What are the signs of the spirit of nature? It is the enemy of mortification. It disregards faith, hope, and love. It quits the interior life at the moment difficulties arrive. It mistakes charity for philanthropy. It has an egoism that cares not about the glory due to God in right worship and has disregard for the salvation of souls. Here, mediocrity passes for virtue.

What is the spirit of the devil? It is one of pride that quickly switches back and forth from presumption to discouragement.

[324] Tanquerey, Very Rev. Adolphe, *The Spiritual Life*, no. 1282–1284.

The devil tempts souls to imitate him who fell through pride. He usually brings temptations which are sudden, violent, and protracted beyond measure.[325]

What are the signs of the spirit of God? God helps souls live the Gospel by remaining faithful to what our holy ancestors and fathers celebrated and by rejecting novelty.[326] Exterior mortifications are done under obedience, not to impress others, and not to the point of ruining one's health. Mortification should beget holy desires, increase our zeal through the prospect of reward. It ought to engender courage, endurance, and the assurance of success.[327]

The spirit of God gives us peace with neighbor, a joy the world cannot take, and a forgetfulness of self. The Holy Ghost takes up His abode in these fervent souls as a Guest, inspiring the simplicity of not bearing any negative thoughts or ill will towards any person.[328] "A dove, a bird which exemplifies the virtue of simplicity, hurts no one, with either its beak or claws."[329] Simplicity is an attribute of God and "arises from seeking one thing alone: the one thing necessary," the Supreme Good.[330]

Now, turn to the prayers to be recited during the *illuminative* way and the Chaplet of the Holy Face (p. 85, 20).

---

325 Tanquerey, Very Rev. Adolphe, *The Spiritual Life*, no. 222.

326 St. Vincent of Lerins, *Commonitorium,* para II, VI.

327 Tanquerey, Very Rev. Adolphe, *The Spiritual Life*, no. 1197–1198.

328 St. Albert the Great, *The Paradise of the Soul*, p. 185.

329 St. Albert the Great, *The Paradise of the Soul*, p. 186.

330 St. Albert the Great, *The Paradise of the Soul*, p. 186.

# Day 20

## The Holy Face before the High Priests

The mock trial arrives. First, Annas and Caiaphas have no true evidence but are only calumniators before the serene Face of Jesus. Their lust for power brings a profound ignorance and jealousy of the true Messiah.

The pontiff questions Jesus on His doctrines. Jesus responds that He has spoken openly to the masses. Then one of the servants standing there gave Jesus a blow. "Why was I not there with my Franks!"[331] exclaimed the young King Clovis on hearing this passage for the first time.

From Annas, let us pass to Caiaphas. Jesus responds with silence to the first question. It is similar to the world today that asks the Church mock questions. Just as Jesus was silent in His passion, silence comes from the mock questions of the world.

In desperation, Caiaphas cries out, asking if He is the Christ. "Thou hast said it," answered Jesus. "Let us admire the sweetness, the serenity, the wisdom of the divine words of Jesus. . . . Annas and Caiaphas belong to all ages; there have always been obscure persecutors and also persecutors *clothed with purple and seated upon thrones of pride and cruelty.*"[332]

The Church, the spouse of Christ, when she imitates the Holy Face, will, like Him, receive the blow of the servant. Priests and faithful of Christ, offer your cheek, for you have also dared to speak the truth to the powerful world. But take courage:

---

[331] Fourault, *The Month of the Holy Face*, pp. 196–97. King Clovis was the first king of the Franks (French). He was baptized in 508.

[332] Fourault, p. 198 (author's emphasis).

Jesus has given us the Holy Sacrifice, Holy Communion, and the Blessed Virgin Mary to make us grow in imitation of Him.

O adorable Face of Jesus, source of grace, light, and peace, grant that we may walk with a firm step, aided by the Mass, Holy Communion, and the Blessed Virgin Mary, along the path of holiness. By often contemplating Thy Effigy, may it impress on our souls the divine resemblance which Thou desirest to see shining on Thy saints.

## The Sacrifice of the Mass and Proficients

The cumulative effect of the Mass is to assist us toward a happy death. It was by the death of the Holy Redeemer that the watershed of graces came to humanity. Proficients should mortify sin and put it to death, like Jesus did. "It was not death which approached Him, it was He who approached death. That is why the Saviour commands the portal of death to open unto Him in the presence of the Father. The chalice is gradually being drained of its rich red wine of salvation."[333] Fruitfully attending Mass will order us to the last act of love here on earth. This act of death may very well open the gates of heaven to us immediately, if well prepared for by our whole life.

The exemplar for our assistance at the Holy Sacrifice is Mary at the foot of the cross. The mystery of the Mass places us next to her, as if we were transported there in time and space. Assistance at Mass also affords us practical lessons which will enable us to prepare ourselves for a good death.

Saint Pius X said, "O Lord, my God, from this moment with a tranquil and submissive heart, I accept from Thy hand

---

[333] Sheen, Archbishop Fulton, *Calvary and the Mass*, p. 65.

the type of death that it shall please Thee to send me, with all its anguish, sufferings and sorrows."

Christ rendered satisfaction to God by His sacrifice. The Savior's sacrifice does not render our sacrifice useless but raises it and gives it its value. Mary is the chief example of this reparation. She offered a divine Person up for sacrifice. She was so reverent that it pleased God to reveal how she received Communion from St. Peter's first Mass. "[S]he was surrounded by heavenly spirits, who were there present, with ineffable respect. Before reaching the altar, the great Queen performed three acts of humility: she prostrated upon the earth, to the edification of the faithful, who were moved to tears."[334]

Jesus prayed for His executioners. The dying man should unite himself to all the Masses being celebrated and forgive all those who persecuted him.

The proficient should make a sacrifice of thanksgiving at Mass for all the benefits received by staying after Mass and making a thanksgiving after Communion from fifteen minutes to an hour, if possible. They should be thankful for crosses. "The Mass is that which makes the Cross visible to every eye; it placards the Cross at all the crossroads of civilization; it brings Calvary so close that even tired feet can make the journey to its sweet embrace; every . . . ear may hear its sweet appeal, for the Mass and the Cross are the same."[335]

What should be the Communion for proficients? Notice in the chart below how Communion and Thanksgiving are part of the unitive way in the Mass. Each Communion should be more fervent than the preceding one. The ascent of the saints

---

[334] Fr. Müller, Michael, *The Holy Sacrifice of the Mass*, p. 355.

[335] Sheen, Archbishop Fulton, *Calvary and the Mass*, p. 59.

was increasingly rapid as they approached nearer to God, the acceleration is far more for proficients than beginners. Communion should increase charity. Fraternal charity is one of the great signs of progress of the love of God.[336]

| **Interior Level** | **Parts of the Mass** |
|---|---|
| Purgative | Confiteor<br>Introit<br>Kyrie<br>Gloria |
| Illuminative | Collect, Epistle,<br>Gospel, Credo, Offertory |
| Unitive | Consecration, Communion,<br>Thanksgiving |

However, proficients may yet have obstacles: mental strain, inordinate desire for consolation, or a false elevation in the mind of their own sanctity. Once they remove these obstacles and ask for generosity to remove them, affective prayer becomes highly conducive to spiritual progress and apostolic zeal.[337] If we are negligent in doing so ourselves, we should ask God to take care of it, no matter how painful it may be.

Holy Communion should contribute to the growth of the mystical body of Jesus. If we do not prepare ourselves to receive Communion ever more perfectly, it will be impossible to reach

[336] See 1 Cor. 10:16.

[337] Tanquerey, Very Rev. Adolphe, *The Spiritual Life*, no. 988.

the unitive way. God will grant the generous heart's desire to taste God in Communion, which is the manna of heaven that shall never die away.

Communion will aid in a more generous gift of oneself and imitation of Our Lord. "The more we empty ourselves of self, the more ready we make the soul to let itself be inhabited and possessed by God."[338] Fervent Communion will give greater generosity, causing the gift of God received to radiate to other souls like the Holy Face of Jesus.

## The Devotion to Mary in Proficients

What is the evidence of devotion to Mary in proficients? It is a promptness of the will in service of God.[339] It was Mary who gave us Jesus, and on the final day, it will be Mary who will give us to Jesus. To neglect mediators that God has given us shows a lack of humility. True devotion to Mary, as practiced by slaves according to the method of Saint Louis de Montfort, will bring rapid intimacy with Our Lord.

Slavery means that we consecrate all our acts, property, merits, and whole being to Mary. She is the best investor of our spiritual goods and a better treasury within which to preserve them from rust, since she was conceived without sin.

What are the fruits of this devotion? It is the surest, easiest, and quickest road to reach Our Lord. Why? Mary supports us with her gentleness, and she can obtain for us a greater charity, which is the principle of merit. Proficients who submit as slaves

338 Tanquerey, Very Rev. Adolphe, *The Spiritual Life*, no. 283.
339 *Summa Theologica* II–II q. 82, a. 1.

to Mary walk giant steps in the interior life because she is the spouse of the Holy Ghost.

At each moment of Communion, we should ask for Mary's assistance. "How we need Mary to help us profit from this ineffable gift! She teaches us to submerge ourselves with her, in her, and in our Jesus, that we may be transformed in Him."[340]

Now, turn to the prayers to be recited during the *illuminative* way and the Chaplet of the Holy Face (p. 85, 20).

# Day 21

## The Holy Face in the Presence of the Executioners

Jesus offers Himself freely to drink the dregs of the chalice of opprobrium when He suffers the unique malice of His executioners. His eyes are first veiled with a bandana; His Face is spit upon, and blasphemy falls upon His sacred ears. Iron gauntlets crush upon His lips and cheeks, whereby blood gushes over His Face. These slaves of Satan shout, "Prophesy unto us, O Christ, who is he that struck thee."[341]

Clothed in a cloak of royal red, His head is crowned with thorns and given blows, making the thorns' sharp points penetrate deeply into His head. His beauty is transformed into the ugliness of leprosy. He is now the most despised and abject of men, at the sight of whom observers shake their heads.

Dear sacred head surrounded by thorns, Your mere words have the power to instantly hurl Your enemies into hell, just

[340] Fr. Gabriel of St. Mary Magdalen, O.C.D., *Divine Intimacy*, no. 183.
[341] Matt. 26:68.

as one look and one word spoken in the Garden of Olives cast them, dazed, down to the ground. But no, the time of justice is reserved for the general judgment, where Thy saints will sit on judgment seats, condemning the abject men of the world.

O Savior Jesus, who didst will to cure the body in order to cure the wounds of souls, cast on us a glance of Thy divine Face, and grant us the grace of both simple prayer and the prayer of quiet, that we may grow in the abandonment and humility necessary to advance to the unitive way of prayer.

## Contemplative Prayer and Its Degrees for Proficients

Saint Francis de Sales teaches three differences between meditation and contemplation in his two works *Treatise on the Love of God*[342] and *Introduction to the Devout Life.*[343]

- 1st Difference: meditation becomes simplified affective prayer which fuses into one act.[344]
- 2nd Difference: meditation considers in minute detail, but contemplation gazes with simplicity on the object that it loves.[345]
- 3rd Difference: mediation is made with effort while contemplation is made with pleasure.[346]

---

[342] Bk. IV, ch. 2, 3, 5, 6, 7.

[343] Part. II, ch. 2.

[344] Meditation prepares for the act of love of God, whereas contemplation follows it.

[345] Treatise 5, Bk. VI, ch. 9.

[346] Treatise 5, Bk. VI, ch. 6.

What does Saint Thomas teach about contemplation? He defines it as an act of the intellect superior to reasoning, a simple view of the truth.[347] And its object is not philosophical contemplation on truth but rather on love of God, sprung from charity.[348] It proceeds from a fervent faith life enlightened by the gifts of the Holy Ghost, especially understanding and wisdom, which render faith penetrating and sweet.[349]

Contemplation can be made analogous to water navigation. Rowers are like meditation; effort is exerted to skim across the sea. Sailors are like contemplation, who rely on the wind of sails to sail across the ocean. Contemplation is thus not acquired but infused. It can also be compared to the soaring of an eagle that looks for the pockets of rising hot air. Once found, the eagle circles in that column and floats to the sun. Concretely, one reading the Gospel for the day comes across a familiar passage illuminated in a way never before penetrated. This is infused contemplation.

How does Saint Teresa of Avila distinguish between acquired recollection and passive recollection? Active recollection is a means by which the soul collects together all the faculties, or senses, and enters within itself. It is an excellent way, like a man who goes by plane instead of walking; the former taking only hours instead of months. Those who practice this prayer almost always keep their eyes shut.[350] Acquired affective prayer becomes prayer of simplicity, which prepares for infused contemplation.[351]

---

[347] *Summa Theologica* II–II, a. 3, 4, 6.

[348] *Summa Theologica* II–II, a. 1; a. 1 at ad 1um.

[349] Cf. *Summa Theologica* II–II, q. 8, a. 1, 2, 4, 6, 7; q. 45, a. 1, 2, 5, 6.

[350] Teresa of Avila, *The Way of Perfection,* ch. 28.

[351] Tanquerey, Very Rev. Adolphe, *The Spiritual Life*, no. 984.

Infused prayer, rather than acquired or "rowing," is supernatural. "There is no occasion to shut the eyes, nor does it depend on anything exterior; involuntarily the eyes suddenly close and solitude is found."[352] By divine assistance, anyone can gain it if they practice the maxims of the virtues up to this point. "His Majesty only bestows this favor to those who have renounced the world . . . [being called] to devote themselves to spiritual things."[353] "Contemplation produces so much light, so much love, and so much virtue that it is rightly called the royal road to perfection."[354] In this state, souls practice all the moral virtues in their highest degree and, in particular, of humility, of conformity to God's will, of holy abandonment, and joy and peace in the midst of severe trials.[355] The soul cannot acquire it like rowers moving over the water, but the Holy Ghost infuses it in the soul like wind in the sails.

What is necessary to advance into infused contemplation? It is sequestering oneself from perishable creatures and demonic interference, perseverance in prayer, carrying our cross, and docility to the Holy Ghost. The fruit is a penetrating and sweet prayer, tasting the mysteries of the Mass, the Incarnation, the Most Blessed Trinity, and the Holy Face of Jesus. Tasting these mysteries is a normal prelude to heaven.

What are the degrees of contemplative prayer in proficients? It is a growing intensity of faith, charity, and gifts of the Holy Ghost. The powers of the soul become more gradually captivated by God and allow for better cooperation with our imagination and a growth in virtue with prayer.

---

352 Teresa of Avila, *The Interior Castle*, 4th Mansion, ch. 3.

353 Teresa of Avila, 4th Mansion, ch. 3.

354 Tanquerey, Very Rev. Adolphe, *The Spiritual Life*, no. 1403.

355 Tanquerey, Very Rev. Adolphe, *The Spiritual Life*, no. 1405.

Saint Teresa[356] presents the four degrees by the analogy of watering a garden:

1. Well and pail drawn by hand—discursive meditation.
2. Well and water well by machine—prayer of quiet.
3. Irrigation by river—virtues flower more vigorously.
4. Rain by God—unitive way.

The progression from one to four depends on humility. It bears heroic promises, burning desires, horror of the world, and a clear view of vanity.[357]

What is the prayer of quiet? Jesus spoke about it as a spring of living water to the Samaritan woman. "The other fountain . . . receives the water from the source itself, which signifies God. . . . They [the celestial waters] appear to dilate and enlarge us internally, and benefit us in an inexplicable manner, nor does even the soul itself understand what it receives."[358] It is sometimes called the prayer of sweet quiet and divine tastes.

What conduct is to be observed? It should be humble abandonment in the hands of God, like a little child in the arms of Jesus. The Holy Ghost inclines the soul to loving silence, and affections gush forth as from a spring.

What is the prayer of simple union? When a soul is faithful to all the duties in the state of life, it is able to carefully listen with docility to the inspirations of the Holy Ghost, called "simple union." It is like running water coming from a river.

---

[356] Teresa of Avila, *Life of Herself*, ch. 15–19.

[357] Teresa of Avila, *Life of Herself*, ch. 18.

[358] Teresa of Avila, *Interior Castle*, 4th Mansion, ch. 2.

Sometimes, like Saint Padre Pio, ecstasy happens, where the exterior senses are suspended. Ecstasy is similar to an artist gazing at a flower who does not hear someone speaking to him.

What are signs of the prayer of union? The soul has deep contrition for sin, like Saint Peter after his denial. It has an ardent zeal to make God known to souls, suffers greatly with the thought of souls descending into hell, and glimpses the sufferings of the Holy Face of Jesus. The martyrs, like Saint Lawrence, often experienced this prayer during their torments.

How does the prayer relate to fervent Communion? Those who make spiritual Communions throughout the day and ask for greater fervor when receiving Holy Communion eventually receive the fruit of extremely vivifying and intimate Holy Communions. "He that eateth my flesh and drinketh my blood abideth in me, and I in him."[359] Saint Thomas expressed it well in the sequence for Corpus Christi, "Sitting at the feast of love, we may see Thee Face to Face."

If we truly grow more fervent at daily Communion, the living flame of charity will always make us aspire higher, even to the end of our journey. The great spiritual writers say that this contemplative prayer is within the reach of everyone if they are willing to follow the way of abnegation and humility. Christ encourages us on: "If any man thirst, let him come to me and drink. Out of his belly shall flow rivers of living water,"[360] "a fountain of water springing up into life everlasting."[361]

Now, turn to the prayers to be recited during the *illuminative* way and the Chaplet of the Holy Face (p. 85, 20).

---

[359] John 6:57.

[360] John 7:37.

[361] John 4:14.

# Day 22

## The Holy Face in the Subterranean Chamber Prays to His Father

After the crown of thorns and the robe are placed on Jesus, the executioners withdraw. Jesus is bound in chains and is left in silence. Behold, He prays to His Father. What does He say? It is not recorded in Scripture. Perhaps He continues what He started in the Garden of Olives.

"Now this is eternal life: That they may know Thee, the only true God, and Jesus Christ, whom Thou has sent. . . . Holy Father, keep them in Thy name whom Thou has given me; that they be one, as we also are."

Meditate on the scene. Jesus has just been betrayed by Judas, suffered the mock trial, received blows and spittle on His Face, a crown of thorns was pressed down into His sacred head, and he was clothed in a mock royal robe. He is not silent. Does He pray for you, dear reader, as He does not pray for the world, but for those given by His Father? Does He secure gifts for you during the bitter chalice of His passion that will enable you to receive the higher levels of the interior life? Yes, dear reader, He prayed for you then, and He does so now, that you will become one with Him in a union of hearts.

Behold, the Blessed Virgin Mary above this dungeon wipes the sacred blood from the scourging. Our Savior was tied to a pillar, and they scourged Him with lion's claws tied to leather on His Holy Face, and He turned, as Saint Gertrude relates, only to receive fresh new scourges by a second soldier on His Face. His mother stands above this subterranean chamber with her ear to the ground and gives her love to Him from afar.

Dear soul, life is full of suffering, but make time for silence in order to address God and the heavenly court so that you may be inspired by Him to suffer meritoriously. It is through adversity that God gives the prize—namely, that you will be one with Him.

Dear Lord Jesus, as Thou prayed in the chamber, pray for me so that I may receive infused contemplation, a prelude to heaven. Never permit me to be separated from Thee. I wish to see Thy Face in glory at the end of time. Give me all the helps I need on this sojourn.

## Infused Contemplation and Prayer

Infused contemplation is the last level of the illuminative way and leads to the unitive way. Theologians call it secret wisdom. The Holy Ghost infuses the soul without the senses realizing it: Sweet, simple, loving, protracted gaze on God and things divine, and of special actual grace which takes possession of us and causes us to act in a passive rather than active manner.[362]

Looking again at the difference between meditation and contemplation might help our understanding. Meditation is in our power. It is like rowers receiving a favorable breeze, yet they must still toil.

On the contrary, infused contemplation is not in our power but comes from the Holy Ghost. By analogy, the impulsion of a favorable wind makes the work of oars unnecessary.

When a soul is progressing but attached to some venial sin, infused contemplation begins, but the gifts of the Holy Ghost intervene only weakly, like on a ship with sails which have not yet been spread.

---

[362] Tanquerey, Very Rev. Adolphe, *The Spiritual Life*, no. 386.

With growth through the purgative and illuminative ways, the power of the Holy Ghost is infused over the soul to the point of it receiving a taste of eternal life. Here, the sails are unfurled, and the wind of the Holy Ghost moves the soul sweetly into a deeper union with God. This happens with such peace that, at times, the soul does not perceive it. Saint Anthony said to Cassian, "There is not perfect prayer if the solitary perceives that he is praying."[363]

Saint Teresa notes three indications of a soul that is intensely united with God.

1. The will alone is seized and held in the prayer of quiet.
2. Then, the intellect moves to simple union.
3. The exterior senses are suspended toward God.

The prayer of quiet generally begins in its arid form and terminates in its sweet form. A great purity of heart is required for contemplation. Now, even advanced souls are subject to many imperfections. For example, the experience, though in a milder form, of a reawakening of the seven capital sins. In order to purify them still more and to prepare them for a higher degree of contemplation, God sends them various trials, which are called passive trials. It is God Himself who causes passive trials, and the soul has but to accept them patiently.[364] Afterward, contemplation becomes much more penetrating in the night of the spirit, when the soul is put to the test of great aridity and strong temptations against faith, hope, and love. Then, virtues

---

[363] Coll. ix, 31.

[364] Tanquerey, Very Rev. Adolphe, *The Spiritual Life*, no. 1420.

and humility become heroic and give the soul over for the next phase: transforming union.

Who is called to this height of contemplation? All souls are called to contemplation in general. If souls dispose themselves to the Holy Ghost, He purifies the theological virtues from all alloy through humiliations. He makes souls understand how to love God for His own sake through His truth, goodness, beauty, mercy, and omnipotence. God grants the height of contemplation to whom He wills.[365] God can give it to privileged souls at their infancy.[366] But ordinarily, God gives it to those who are detached and have purity of heart, mind, and intention.[367] The end of the interior and the mystical life is eternal life, the Beatific Vision.

How ought souls be directed to contemplation? Tell souls the grandeur of faith, which inclines one to see things from God's point of view. Encourage souls to move with the speed of the Holy Ghost. The essential element of infused contemplation is passivity, which means that the soul is led, acted upon, moved, directed by the Holy Ghost and does not lead itself, but permits its freedom of activity.[368]

When the proximate call arrives, souls should read the three signs given by Saint John of the Cross.[369] These three will keep souls from derailment during the aridity of the night of the senses:

---

[365] Tanquerey, Very Rev. Adolphe, *The Spiritual Life*, no. 1407.

[366] Tanquerey, Very Rev. Adolphe, *The Spiritual Life*, no. 1408.

[367] Tanquerey, Very Rev. Adolphe, *The Spiritual Life*, no. 1409–1412.

[368] Tanquerey, Very Rev. Adolphe, *The Spiritual Life*, no. 1409–1401.

[369] John of the Cross, *The Dark Night of the Soul*, Bk. 1, ch. 9.

1. We find no comfort in the things of God (i.e., no more sensible consolations but the cross).
2. The memory dwells ordinarily on God with a painful anxiety and carefulness; the soul thinks it is not serving God but going backwards.
3. The inability to meditate and make reflections as before, because God begins now to communicate Himself not by sense but pure spirit.

Contemplation is the hidden manna[370] given by God to generous souls. It is like a dew which makes the virtues grow, which nourishes them, and from which they obtain their crowning perfection: a prelude to the Beatific Vision.[371]

Now, turn to the prayers to be recited during the *illuminative* way and the Chaplet of the Holy Face (p. 85, 20).

---

[370] See St. John Apoc. 2:17.

[371] Tanquerey, Very Rev. Adolphe, *The Spiritual Life*, no. 1417.

# Last Theme: Unitive Way

## Prayers to Be Recited During the Unitive Way

### Litany of the Holy Face

*In reparation for blasphemies, and so implore of God by the adorable Face of His Son the conversion of blasphemers.*

Lord, have mercy on us.
**Christ, have mercy on us.**
Lord, have mercy on us.
Christ, hear us.
Christ, graciously hear us.
Holy Virgin Mary, pray for us.

O adorable Face, which was adored with profound respect by Mary and Joseph when they saw Thee for the first time, **have mercy on us.**

O adorable Face, which in the Stable of Bethlehem didst ravish with joy the angels, the shepherds and the Magi, **have mercy on us.**

O adorable Face, which in the Temple didst transpierce with a dart of love the saintly old man Simeon and the prophetess Anna, **have mercy on us.**

O adorable Face, which was bathed in tears in Thy holy infancy, **have mercy on us.**

O adorable Face, which, when Thou didst appear
in the Temple at twelve years of age,
didst fill with admiration the Doctors of the law,
O adorable Face, white with purity and ruddy with charity,
O adorable Face, more beautiful than the sun, more
lively than the moon, more brilliant than the stars,
O adorable Face, fresher than the roses of spring,
O adorable Face, more precious than gold,
silver, and diamonds,
O adorable Face, whose charms are so ravishing,
and whose grace is so attractive,
O adorable Face, whose every feature is
characterized by nobility,
O adorable Face, contemplated by angels,
O adorable Face, sweet delectation of the Saints,
O adorable Face, masterpiece of the Holy Ghost,
in which the Eternal Father is well pleased,
O adorable Face, delight of Mary and of Joseph,
O adorable Face, ineffable mirror of the
Divine perfections,
O adorable Face, whose beauty is always
ancient and always new,
O adorable Face, which appeases the wrath of God,
O adorable Face, which makest the devils tremble,
O adorable Face, treasure of graces and of blessings,
O adorable Face, exposed in the desert to the
inclemencies of the weather,
O adorable Face, scorched with the heat of the
sun and bathed with sweat in Thy journeys,
O adorable Face, whose expression is all divine,
O adorable Face, whose modesty and sweetness
attracted both the just and sinners,

**have mercy on us.**

O adorable Face, which gavest a holy kiss to the little children, after having blessed them,
O adorable Face, troubled and weeping at the tomb of Lazarus,
O adorable Face, brilliant as the sun and radiant with glory on Mount Tabor,
O adorable Face, sorrowful at the sight of Jerusalem and shedding tears on that ungrateful city,
O adorable Face, bowed to the earth, in the Garden of Olives, and covered with confusion for our sins,
O adorable Face, bathed in a bloody sweat,
O adorable Face, kissed by the traitor Judas,
O adorable Face, whose sanctity and majesty smote the soldiers with fear and cast them to the ground,
O adorable Face, struck by a vile servant, shamefully blindfolded, and profaned by the sacrilegious hands of Thine enemies,
O adorable Face, defiled with spittle and bruised by innumerable buffets and blows,
O adorable Face, whose Divine look wounded the heart of Peter with a dart of sorrow and love,
O adorable Face, humbled for us at the tribunals of Jerusalem,
O adorable Face, which didst preserve Thy serenity when Pilate pronounced the fatal sentence,
O adorable Face, covered with sweat and blood, and falling in the mire under the heavy weight of the Cross,
O adorable Face, worthy of all our respect, veneration, and worship,
O adorable Face, wiped with a veil by a pious woman on the road to Calvary,

**have mercy on us.**

O adorable Face, raised on the instrument of most shameful punishment,
O adorable Face, whose brow was crowned with thorns,
O adorable Face, whose eyes were filled with tears of blood,
O adorable Face, into whose mouth was poured gall and vinegar,
O adorable Face, whose hair and beard were plucked out by the executioners,
O adorable Face, which was made like to that of a leper,
O adorable Face, whose incomparable beauty was obscured under the dreadful cloud of the sins of the world,
O adorable Face, covered with the sad shades of death,
O adorable Face, washed and anointed by Mary and the holy women and wrapped in a shroud,
O adorable Face, enclosed in the sepulcher,
O adorable Face, all resplendent with glory and beauty on the day of the Resurrection,
O adorable Face, all dazzling with light at the moment of Thy Ascension,
O adorable Face, hidden in the Eucharist,
O adorable Face, which wilt appear at the end of time in the clouds with great power and majesty,
O adorable Face, which wilt cause sinners to tremble,
O adorable Face, which wilt fill the just with joy for all eternity,

**have mercy on us.**

Lamb of God, who takest away the sins of the world,
**spare us, O Lord.**
Lamb of God, who takest away the sins of the world,
**graciously hear us.**
Lamb of God, who takest away the sins of the world,
**have mercy on us.**

*Prayer*

I salute Thee, I adore Thee, and I love Thee, O Jesus, my Savior, outraged anew by blasphemers, and I offer Thee, through the heart of Thy blessed Mother, the worship of all the Angels and Saints, as an incense and a perfume of sweet odor, most humbly beseeching Thee, by the virtue of Thy sacred Face, to repair and renew in me and in all men Thy image disfigured by sin. Amen.

## Offering of the Holy Face to the Eternal Father by Venerable Leo DuPont

Almighty God, Eternal Father, contemplate the Face of Thy Son, Our Lord Jesus Christ. We present it to Thee with confidence for the glory of Thy Holy Name, for the exaltation of Thy holy Church, and for the salvation of the world. Most merciful Advocate, He opens His mouth to plead our cause; listen to His cries, behold His tears, O my God, and Thou wilt be touched with compassion towards the poor sinners who ask of Thee grace and mercy. Amen.

## Praises of the Holy Face

Blessed be Jesus!
Blessed be the Holy Face of Jesus!
Blessed be the Holy Face in the majesty and beauty of its heavenly features!
Blessed be the Holy Face through the words which issued from its divine mouth!
Blessed be the Holy Face through all the glances which escaped from its adorable eyes!
Blessed be the Holy Face in the Transfiguration of Tabor!

Blessed be the Holy Face in the fatigues of its apostolate!
Blessed be the Holy Face in the bloody sweat of the agony!
Blessed be the Holy Face in the humiliations of the Passion!
Blessed be the Holy Face in the sufferings of death!
Blessed be the Holy Face in the splendor of the Resurrection!
Blessed be the Holy Face in the glory of light eternal!

## Aspiration

Eternal Father, we offer Thee the adorable Face of Thy well-beloved Son for the honor and glory of Thy holy Name and for the salvation of all men. (Sister Marie de Saint-Pierre.)

# Day 23

## The Holy Face in the Dust of the Road

Our commander-in-chief hastens to victory, laden with the heavy cross. The triumph of the holy cross is about to bring division in the kingdom of hell. The devil who tempted Jesus in the desert will soon discover that the cross is the great victory of the Redeemer and, after its triumph, will notice that his power will be greatly diminished.

Lo, He falls three times, keeping us in suspense, but He arises three times on the road which leads to certain victory. What does He think each time His forehead lay prostrate in the dust, mingled with His sacred Blood? He falls three times to show us, when we are discouraged, that we have to get up each time and go forward through the three conversions in the interior life. He thought of us during His carrying of the cross and prayed to His Father for each of us to have final perseverance, that we might cross the line of death in the state of grace, an assurance of eternal life.

But now, supported by our warrior king, who conquered death for us, we have all the means to continue on the interior life and learn of the way of Our Lord into the unitive way of contemplation.

O most Holy Redeemer, each time Thou risest up, look upon me with the beautiful rays of Thy Holy Face. May Thy look inspire me to continue on the royal road of suffering Thou hast placed in front of me. O Holy Ghost, prepare me to be disposed to passively receive an increase of Thy Holy Gifts. Please grant me perseverance in prayer and final perseverance.

## Description of Night of the Spirit, Entrance into the Unitive Way

The first conversion, which requires the action of generosity, mortification, and abandonment to Divine Providence, brings the soul into the purgative way. The second conversion requires the passive purification of the senses, leading to the illuminative way, like the apostles, especially Peter on the night of the Passion. The third and last conversion demands the passive purification of the spirit, leads the soul into the unitive way, and transforms the soul like the apostles when they received the Holy Ghost at Pentecost.

This final night gives a more profound and radical purification to proficients so they will be ready to enter the spiritual marriage.[372] When the soul passes through this stage, it has the disposition to receive the Beatific Vision without passing

[372] Tanquerey, Very Rev. Adolphe, *The Spiritual Life*, no. 1463.

through purgatory. Although this summit is rare and lofty, it is not extraordinary, like the gift of prophecy, but is the ordinary way of sanctifying grace in the soul. This is expressed by charity, uniting one to God until death, which brings about eternal life.

Why is passive purification necessary? Saint Thomas uses the analogy in Saint John's Gospel of the good branch that must be pruned. The natural branch has too many shoots, thus yielding less fruit because sap loses its efficacy by excessive diffusion in these superfluous shoots; therefore, the vinedresser prunes them. Something similar happens to the generous soul who is involved in so many exterior practices that the strength of the interior life is diminished. The good Lord prunes His good servants and cuts away what is useless so they may bear more fruit. The Lord inures them to battle, and this further purifies so they mature in virtue and become proportionately richer in good works.

These are passive purifications received from God, unlike the mortification a just man imposes on himself. God trains souls to live the life of a soldier, like the apostles who crowned their lives with martyrdom.

"For gold and silver are tried in fire, but acceptable men in the furnace of humiliation."[373] This passive purification of the spirit prepares the soul for close union with God.

What are the defects of the advanced? They need to see the value of the cross in the midst of the unreasonable troubles which they foolishly create. Any remaining imperfections must be plucked up as bad roots imbedded in the depth of the soul, which the purification of the senses could not reach. For instance, friendships which are a bit too ardent, and other

[373] Ecclus. 2:5.

distractions from within and attractions from without which create a certain dullness of mind.[374] Advanced souls may still have moments of rudeness, impatience, and bitter zeal, which leads them to sermonize their neighbor and to deliver untimely remonstrances. "Some of them become so entangled in manifold falsehoods and delusions, and so persist in them that their return to the pure road of virtue and real spirituality is exceedingly doubtful."[375]

These souls, although proficients, still lack justice and charity, which shows in their relations with superiors, equals, and inferiors. They are too attached to their own judgment. They may have a certain pride or a vain self-complacency resulting from the abundance of spiritual consolations received. They may have illusions and mistake false visions and prophecies for true ones. They have an over-boldness toward God and lose that reverential fear of Him, which is a safeguard to virtue.[376] St. John of the Cross says this purification is wrought through the light of infused contemplation, a light bright in itself, but dim and painful to the soul on account of the latter's ignorance and impurity.[377]

We must be disposed to renounce our plans, our projects, and our views, not only regarding material things, but even spiritual ones, for we must go to God not by a way of our own choosing or taste but only by the way which He Himself has prepared for us. We must be disposed to renounce divine consolations and to walk in darkness and aridity for as long as

---

[374] Tanquerey, Very Rev. Adolphe, *The Spiritual Life*, no. 1464.

[375] John of the Cross, *The Dark Night of the Soul*, Bk. II, ch. 2.

[376] Tanquerey, Very Rev. Adolphe, *The Spiritual Life*, no. 1464.

[377] Tanquerey, Very Rev. Adolphe, *The Spiritual Life*, no. 1465.

Our Lord wills, to renounce our most cherished works, our most legitimate affections, our most holy friendships, even the very support of the one who understands and guides us in the way of God.[378]

Saint Augustine and Saint Louis of Bertrand prayed often, "Lord, burn, cut, do not spare on this earth, that Thou mayest spare in eternity."

How deep must the will be purified? There is an unconscious egoism that leads to a constant conversation with oneself. The purification of this night leads a soul from fruitless monologue to a constant, tranquilizing, and vivifying conversation with God. This egoism is manifested when trial strikes: the soul becomes upset, seeking consolation from without, committing petty sins and prevalent faults. The only way to overcome this is to let God take complete possession and occupy our interior.

The poor in spirit, once refined and stripped of self, receive the light[379] of Jesus. The leaders of the Church, Pharisees, princes, and the High Priest did not follow the Lord, but ironically, the common people did. Those who should have led put Him to death. "Far from taking the initiative, the only option left to the poor in spirit is to accept with love, to endure with patience and humility all that God disposes for us."[380] Thus, certain souls need to be convinced that God disposes all for the good of those who love Him. The soul of faith sees in every person a messenger from our Lord, charged by Him to exercise

---

[378] Fr. Gabriel of St. Mary Magdalen, O.C.D., *Divine Intimacy*, no. 349.

[379] See John 1:5. "The light shines in the darkness, and the darkness did not comprehend it."

[380] Fr. Gabriel of St. Mary Magdalen, O.C.D., *Divine Intimacy*, no. 351.

in it virtue, particularly in that which it lacks most.[381] Tauler suggests asking that the true light may shine through any spiritual blindness. It behooves the soul at this point to attach itself to those who are attached to God.

The passive purification will certainly not be without suffering. Saint Camille of Verano gave striking words: "Feel bitter pain for [sufferings God] did not predispose to send you because of your ingratitude and your little spirit, and you should know that it is out of charity that he would like to give you every bad thing in order to have a reason to give you every good thing."[382]

With generosity, the light of God will shine on the soul completely, and hence the light of Baptism will grow until the entrance into heaven. Since charity corresponds to the gift of wisdom, it proceeds from contemplation into union with God.

What happens in the passive purification of the spirit? The soul is deprived of the lights it once received. Note that this is exacted by God and is not due to sufferings which result from a person's lack of virtue. The soul became too familiar with these lights and saw them in a too human way. Mary Magdalen did this when she saw Jesus at the Resurrection, and Jesus asked her not to hold Him. God withholds from the soul the former sweetness it had for spiritual things.[383] So the loss is not only a sensible aridity but the spiritual lights which it once received. Souls now have to walk in darkness by pure faith, like the apostles after the deprivation of Christ after His ascension. This was a profound solitude, like a desert. It resembles a parishioner returning to normal life after a holy priest has finished a parish

---

381 Fr. Gabriel of St. Mary Magdalen, O.C.D., *Divine Intimacy*, no. 351.

382 Varano, *Life and Writings*, p. 80.

383 John of the Cross, *Dark Night of the Soul*, Bk. II, ch. 3.

mission. The apostles were attached to the humanity of Christ and so had to be purified by His absence and prepared to receive the Holy Ghost, who would strengthen them.

How is God revealed in this darkness? It is like when the sun has disappeared, and we are able to see further the stars at night. Thus, when Christ ascended, the apostles were able to grasp His majesty. Temptations in this third conversion are against faith and hope, whereas in the second conversion, they are against chastity and patience. In this darkness, generous souls suffer greatly from the sight of sin or the thought of souls going to hell. This suffering disposes them to a profound contemplation of the infinite goodness of God.

At the beginning, souls suffer small spiritual or temporal suffering, but once they reach the summit, they find the purest suffering, without admixture of consolation.[384] "Tauler says that the Holy Ghost creates a void in the depth of our souls where egoism and pride still dwell. He creates the void that He may heal us, and then He fills it to overflowing while continually increasing our capacity to receive."[385]

Saint Teresa speaks of the passive purification as the sixth mansion in *The Interior Castle*.

We must pass through this crucible of suffering in order to have a concept of our Savior's passion and of His humility, after which an experienced love of the cross brings true sanctity.

Now, turn to the prayers to be recited during the *unitive* way and the Chaplet of the Holy Face (p. 159, 20).

---

[384] Paul of the Cross, Letters, I, 153.

[385] Tauler, Second Sermon for Pentecost.

# Day 24

## The Holy Face of Jesus Given to Veronica

Members of the confraternities of the Holy Face have a keen interest in Saint Veronica because she broke through the mob of soldiers and the sarcasm of the common people to console the Face of Jesus.

It was a custom for women to give their veil to guests so they could wipe their faces to remove dust and sweat. One account recalls Saint Veronica, also known as Serapha,[386] wearing a veil on her head and carrying one on her left arm. She was most likely a close disciple of Jesus, so she braved the crowd, unlike the apostles, and waited for Jesus to approach on His way of the cross.

She weaved through the gap as Jesus fell, stunning the Roman soldiers in their tracks. The guards did not know what to do, seeing such bravery and compassion for a condemned man. With the calm like in the eye of a hurricane, Jesus looked up, having no longer the appearance of a man. Saint Veronica took the fine Egyptian linen veil and wiped His Face on it. After a full moment of peace, the guards violently moved them on.

Jesus turned to the crowd of weeping women and told them, "Weep not over me, but weep for yourselves and for your children."[387]

Veronica, without looking at the soiled veil, wrapped it over her left arm and ran home with one of the other weeping women. When they arrived at home, Veronica hurriedly placed

---

[386] In one of her visions, Blessed Anne Catherine Emmerich mentions the pious woman as "Serapha."

[387] Luke 23:28.

the linen on the table and went to the corner to weep. Her companion looked at the veil and rejoiced and picked it up. She turned it to Veronica, who saw the impression of the Redeemer for the first time. She remarked that she was not worthy for her Lord to leave her such a precious remembrance of His Countenance. Later, she gave the veil to Saint Clement I, after showing it to the princes of this world.

O Lord, it is the generous souls to whom Thou give the greatest rewards. Veronica, intercede for me so that I will always break through the mob of temptation and never be separated from my Lord. Lord, make me generous in my spiritual life, and then Thou will show Thy Face to me as a foretaste of heaven.

## The Cause of the Passive Purification and Transluminous Obscurity

Souls moving through the unitive way gradually understand their great poverty and wretchedness. Saint Alphonsus wrote that these souls who have committed even just one mortal sin deserve eternal punishment, but God's ways are merciful and deep. As the soul moves through the levels of wretchedness, a purifying light and spiritual fire rids it of its stains.

The melting point of silver is 1,763°F,[388] and it is purified in a crucible with an intense material fire. A more intense fire is needed to transform coal into a diamond; likewise, the just man needs to be purified by an intense spiritual fire.

"O my God enlighten my darkness."[389] At first this light is obscure and inflicts pain, revealing to the soul only its miseries;

[388] 961°C.

[389] Ps. 17:29.

but once imperfections have been eliminated through sorrow, it reveals the riches to be gained and thus becomes a source of consolation.[390] When a soul is asked, "Do you wish to be purified?" and gives the correct response, the Holy Ghost does a profound work, delivering it from the self-love which often blinds it. Know this is a purifying light and do not flee from it on account of fear of the truth about oneself.

For example, the Curé of Ars considered the loftiness of the priesthood but thought himself yet ever further from its ideal. Or Saint Padre Pio, who said people making pilgrimage to see him hindered his work of hearing confessions. These were souls considered very holy by the Church, but they considered themselves as nothing. The same sentiments must prevail in souls who approach the unitive way by profound humility.

When fire catches onto a log, it first blackens it; then it turns white at the end. When the soul enters the beginning stages of the unitive way, its condition is apparently worse than it was before. The black rivers of Florida are saturated with tannins. In this stage, one can see more clearly the blights on their souls, as one cannot see the tannins in the "black river" of Florida until one enters into it more deeply.

Doctors speak of a healing crisis when the patient goes through intense pain as it is being cured. This is a salutary crisis, a purgatory before death. "And thus," says Saint John of the Cross, "the soul which passes through this state in the present life, and is perfectly purified, either enters not into purgatory, or is detained there but a moment, for one hour here is of greater moment than many there."[391] And remember: suffering here

---

[390] Tanquerey, Very Rev. Adolphe, *The Spiritual Life*, no. 1468.

[391] John of the Cross, *The Dark Night of the Soul,* Bk. II, ch. 10.

has merit, but not so in purgatory. "In reality, however, rare are they who go immediately from earth to heaven."[392]

How does the gift of understanding change in this purification? The Holy Ghost moves the mind of the soul from common sense of things toward a divine sense, and the soul is at times carried out of itself. The light of understanding is strengthened; thus, the mind can penetrate more deeply into the essence of things. The precondition of a perfect understanding is faith united to charity. "St. John of the Cross explains at length how this work of purification is accomplished by the Holy Spirit, who invading the soul with the living flame of His Love, destroys and consumes all its imperfections."[393] The deep things of God are gradually incorporated into one's scope. During strong temptations, like a lightning flash, consideration on death and hell are presented. "Blessed are the clean of heart" is the beatitude dealt with here. The soul enters into a higher plane of obscurity, going deeper into knowledge of its great poverty, culpability, and wretchedness. It recognizes more the great majesty of God and its own nothingness, which, after this night, is a prelude to spiritual marriage. "The more deeply convinced we are that purification is the work of Love, the more eager we shall be to welcome it gladly, and to embrace it courageously even when it costs us dear."[394] "The night of the spirit thus appears as the normal prelude of eternal life and as its painful germination in us."[395]

---

[392] See "The Number of the Saved" by Saint Leonard of Port Maurice.

[393] Tanquerey, Very Rev. Adolphe, *The Spiritual Life*, no. 1062–1063.

[394] Fr. Gabriel of St. Mary Magdalen, O.C.D., *Divine Intimacy*, no. 348.

[395] Mystics call it transluminous obscurity because of its great darkness when viewed on this side of heaven.

What is the transluminous obscurity? It is too great a light. God seems dark to us because we cannot attain a view of His Essence. God's ways are deep for us, and His providence has a wonderful harmonization of infinite justice, infinite mercy, and supreme liberty in the mystery of predestination. This seems obscure to souls at this stage, and they are tempted on the subject of predestination. Souls in the dark night think they are backsliding when, in reality, they are progressing. They must make great acts of faith. The Holy Trinity seems obscure because the eyes of the spirit are too weak. Christ's passion caused all but one of the apostles to flee, but this was the very moment of victory.

Souls struggle with maintaining that God is good because they suffer so greatly. Souls are beleaguered with a fear of having consented to temptation, as was Holy Job. Saint Alphonsus Liguori thought his order, the Redemptorists, would perish. But perseverance will give souls a soft light that will be met with again on leaving this tunnel.[396] This night of the soul is a mystical death which establishes a deeper humility, in a purer and more perfect hope, because now the soul trusts only in the merciful love of God.[397] During the night of the spirit, the inferior lights are taken away so the soul can see the heights of the spiritual firmament.[398]

How is the soul to act? Act like the woman of Canaan. She persevered and was persistent: It seemed the woman of Canaan was not heard by Christ when she prayed to Him. She humbled herself when the Lord challenged her. "Yea, Lord; for the

[396] John of the Cross, *The Dark Night of the Soul*, Bk. I, ch. 7.
[397] Fr. Gabriel of St. Mary Magdalen, O.C.D., *Divine Intimacy*, no. 353.
[398] *Summa Theologica* II–II, q. 180, a. 6.

whelps also eat of the crumbs that fall from the table of their masters. Then Jesus answering, said to her: O woman, great is thy faith."[399]

"In proportion as a man renounces himself and goes out of himself; in the same proportion God enters into him in very truth."[400]

Now, turn to the prayers to be recited during the *unitive* way and the Chaplet of the Holy Face (p. 159, 20).

# Day 25

## The Holy Face upon the Cross

The frenzy of the demons is manifest in the executioners as they seize the cross and raise it high. Candidates of total consecration to the Holy Face and friends of reparation, let us attach ourselves especially to the contemplation of the suffering of the Holy Face.

Christ our King wears a mock crown, which the executioners wove to symbolize His real royalty. Fastened upon the new Tree of Life, His suffering was such that He did not know where to repose His head without augmenting the cruel sufferings. Make reparation for His suffering sense of touch.[401]

Christ, Thy ears are torn by the blasphemies of the people. "Let Christ the king of Israel come down now from the cross,

---

[399] Matt. 15:27–28.

[400] Tauler, *Sermons* (Trans. Hugueny) I, 241 ff.

[401] Note that the Chaplet of the Holy Face makes reparation for Our Lord's five senses.

that we may see and believe."[402] Make reparation for His suffering sense of hearing.

Christ, Thine eyes are filled with tears of blood, and Thou weepest over our sins, the sight of which, like a fearful cloud, obscures the incomparable beauty of Thy august Face. Let us make reparation for His suffering sense of sight.

Christ, Thou thirst for souls falling into hell, saying, *Sitio*! "I thirst!" They bring gall mixed with vinegar to quench Thy thirst, and after tasting it, Thou turn away Thy adorable Face from the sour mixture. Let us make reparation for the suffering of His last two senses of taste and smell.

It is through the senses that the devil enters our souls; it is by them that reparation ought to be accomplished. "At the sight of His ears torn by blasphemy, who would not hasten to close his own to flattery, to licentious conversation, to backbiting, to calumnies, to criticizing his neighbor?"[403]

"Oh amiable Face of my Jesus, I adore and I love Thee. I detest my pride, which has crowned Thee with thorns, my sensuality, which has torn Thee by the hands of the executioners; my love of independence which, during three hours, has kept Thee attached to the Cross."[404] I make reparation for these my vices and beg Thy Divine Majesty to give me the conduct required to observe the purification of my spirit by generous acceptance of suffering, faith in the mystery of the cross, and the love of submission and conformity to God's good pleasure.

---

[402] Mark 15:32.

[403] Fourault, *The Month of the Holy Face*, p. 238.

[404] Fourault, p. 239.

## Conduct to Be Observed During the Purification of the Spirit

The passive purification spoken of in the preceding chapter is a purifying light which chiefly increases the gift of understanding. The following shall guide the soul with rules of direction in this state of often prolonged aridity, which sometimes is so painful.

The general rule is to treat yourself with kindness. The great commandment requires love of oneself in an ordinate way. The first rule is to accept this trial generously for as long as God permits it. Because of love, these souls are neither frightened nor alarmed; their ideal is divine union, and they desire to reach it at any cost. No sacrifice seems too hard, provided it reaches the goal.[405] One of the best books for further reading is *Abandonment to Divine Providence* by Father De Caussade, SJ. The two common errors of control and despair can be overcome by:

1. cooperating with God and
2. persevering in prayer.

The latter can be accomplished by asking God for perseverance in prayer, faith, trust, and love. If one continues to pray, it is a sign that God is still helping; for no one can continue to pray without a new actual grace.

Does faith in the mystery of the cross help during this purification? Yes, the cross has a great efficacy. It is necessary and good for us.

The cross renders suffering sweet as St. Francis declares: "So great is the good which awaits me that all pain is delightful

[405] Fr. Gabriel of St. Mary Magdalen, O.C.D., *Divine Intimacy*, no. 347.

to me."[406] The experience of suffering with merit gives us an understanding of the mystery of the cross in a more profound and living way.

The Christian who carries his cross displays the distinctive sign of configuration to our Redeemer, a sign of predestination characterized by these attributes:

1. Patience in adversity for the love of God.
2. Love of enemies in spite of their insults and calumnies.
3. Love of the poor, especially when personal affliction supernaturally inclines us to help them.[407]

During this stage, hope grows in the soul through constant prayer. Upon waking, ask God for the grace of perseverance in prayer. If this is done daily, the grace to pray constantly is granted, even if it sometimes takes many years. The daily examination of conscience is a great time to ask: Have I kept my daily prayer promises? When we pray, even when it is most difficult, the soul will desire God more and more purely and *strongly.*

Why is it important to be completely abandoned to God's divine providence or His good pleasure? It is during spiritual tribulations and afflictions that the soul can nourish itself with the will of God, "Thy will be done." It is imperative to place all confidence in Him, for He is with us all our days, even in dark days, when the horizon is black without any ray of light, when the enemy seems to triumph, when our friends forsake us, and when, humanly speaking, one does not see any possibilities of success.[408]

---

[406] Fr. Gabriel of St. Mary Magdalen, O.C.D., *Divine Intimacy*, no. 347.
[407] Garrigou-Lagrange, p. 395.
[408] Fr. Gabriel of St. Mary Magdalen, O.C.D., *Divine Intimacy*, no. 335.

At this point, the soul must continually grow in the beatitudes, for the reward is great on earth and in heaven. He will receive the hundredfold of close union with God over and above all that is taken from him, and also secure the salvation of souls. Memorizing pertinent biblical phrases like, "If God be for us who is against us?"[409] helps the soul grow deeper in blessed conformity to Him.

Ask the Lord for a love of the cross and a desire to share in His holy humiliations, in the measure willed by Providence. The *Imitation* illustrates the royal road of the cross:

> In the cross is salvation; in the cross is life; in the cross is protection from enemies. In the cross is an infusion of heavenly sweetness; in the cross is strength of mind; in the cross is joy of spirit; in the cross is height of virtue; in the cross is perfection of sanctity. . . . No man hath so heartfelt a sense of the passion of Christ as he whose lot it hath been to suffer like things. . . . If thou carry the cross willingly, it will carry thee. . . . If thou carry it unwillingly, thou makest it a burden to thee, and loadest thyself the more. . . . For the sufferings of this life are not worthy to be compared with the glory to come.[410]

Thus, suffering well removes pride, and the void it creates makes the soul increasingly capable of receiving divine grace.

Now, turn to the prayers to be recited during the *unitive* way and the Chaplet of the Holy Face (p. 159, 20).

---

[409] Rom. 8:31.

[410] Thomas à Kempis, *The Imitation of Christ*, Bk. II, ch. 12, passion.

# Day 26

## The Holy Face and Saint Dismas

During the Holy Sacrifice of the Mass, the Christian is transported to the scene of the Crucifixion. Behold Jesus hanging on the infamous gibbet and the two thieves, one on His right and one on His left.

Blasphemies continue to spew, once from the crowd, thence from the executioners, and then, most grievously, from the priests. But wait, one of the thieves blasphemes too: "If thou be Christ, save thyself and us."[411] How easy it must have been to see Jesus, unrecognizable, worse than a leper, dying the death of a criminal.

Then, Saint Dismas defends Our Lord with words of reparation. "Neither dost thou fear God, seeing thou art under the same condemnation? And we indeed justly, for we receive the due reward of our deeds; but this man hath done no evil."[412] According to Saint John Chrysostom, Saint Dismas had greater faith than Abraham, Moses, and Isaiah, "They," he says, "saw Christ upon the throne and in the bosom of his glory and they believed; he sees him in the midst of torments, and he adores him as though he were in glory; he sees him on the cross and he prays to him as though he were seated in the highest heavens; he sees a criminal, and he invokes a king."[413]

Who cannot admit that we are all thieves and wretches, having committed sin, but we are still here. God, in His mercy, has given us the chance to endure the passive purification so

---

411 Luke 23:39.

412 Luke 23:40–41.

413 Janvier, *Manual of the Archconfraternity of the Holy Face*, pp. 77–78.

we can have a greater faith like Saint Dismas, who heard these words from Jesus, "Amen, I say to you, today you will be with me in paradise."[414]

Dear Holy Face of Jesus, Thou showed Thy sweet Face to Saint Dismas, and he uttered the consoling words of reparation that wound the Father's heart like golden arrows, pouring out torrents of mercy. Give us great generosity like Saint Dismas, so we may bear the purification of the spirit generously. After arriving at the end of purification, we beg Thee for one of its effects: the special gift of final perseverance.

## The Effects of the Passive Purification

What happens to a soul that goes through the passive purification, the third and last test? God wants the advantage of souls. He purifies them by darkening the mind to give it light, humbling it to raise it up, impoverishing it to give it divine possession.[415] Two things happen to these souls; first, defects are suppressed, and second, the virtues in the elevated part of the soul are perfected, chiefly humility and the theological virtues.

What defects are removed? Distractions, dullness of spirit, need for consolation, self-love, subtle egoism; all these gradually disappear. "The soul sees sufferings as more profitable than joy because it develops a firm determination to do nothing that might offend God."[416] During temptation, the soul moves into the center of itself where God dwells, and temptation becomes an opportunity for great merit, for Saint Thomas believes that

---

[414] Luke 23:43.

[415] Tanquerey, Very Rev. Adolphe, *The Spiritual Life*, no. 1467.

[416] Tanquerey, Very Rev. Adolphe, *The Spiritual Life*, no. 1468.

our conscience is that place where intimate secrets of the heart cannot escape to the enemy.[417]

The soul becomes more kind to his neighbor, where rudeness, impatience, and ambition once ruled. The soul is willing to help the poor even if it is greatly suffering. A true zeal, as opposed to a bitter zeal, grows. Souls are attractive, like the saints, because they draw patience, gentleness, and disinterestedness from the life of God. All persecutions are seen as opportunities to draw profit. True sanctity is the result of generously enduring persecution.

Collective trials, like God sending the scourge of revolutionary men to punish the world for blasphemy and irreverence, distinguish the true servants of God. The Lord visits the world in progressive stages of consolation, chastisement, and finally condemnation. Souls in the unitive way excel under the conditions of the latter two. When they speak, they impart peace because, by wisdom, they see the trial as God sees it. "We assume other persons' crosses are lighter, forgetful that the reason our cross is hard is simply because it is our own. Our Lord did not make his Cross; it was made for him. So yours is made by the circumstances of your life, and by your routine duties. That is why it fits so tightly."[418]

What happens to the virtues? Humility, piety, and the theological virtues are greatly purified of all human dross.[419] To drive out pride and all human respect, the Lord Himself must intervene by giving understanding and knowledge so that our wretchedness throws light on the hidden folds in the con-

---

[417] *Summa Theologica* I, q. 57, a. 4.

[418] Sheen, Archbishop Fulton, *The Cross and the Crib*, p. 40.

[419] When silver is purified, the impurities removed are called dross.

science, in which lie the seeds of death.[420] Humility of heart reaches its zenith, which loves to be nothing so that God may be all. This humility sees how easy it is to lose salvation and thus possesses a great desire for the special gift to persevere to the end, which is called final perseverance.

All the saints possessed great humility and were thus very attractive. True piety was their lot, which is a promptness to the service of the Lord, especially in the absence of sensible devotion.[421]

Since this purification is a test of faith, the effect on generous souls is an unmovable faith. The devil tempts the soul to believe in the severity of inexorable divine justice, as if the damned sought pardon but were unable to obtain it. Whereas these purified souls seek pardon, in reality, damned souls never ask pardon. When tempted against faith, these souls also recognize the truth of divine justice, because God has revealed it, but it does not lead them to despair. They also see that God's permission of the greatest evils is holy and brings about the greatest good. At the end of the third conversion, faith is increased exponentially. The only reality that counts is supernatural life, and souls here ask themselves whether they will be able to persevere.

Hope is also purified. Hope is the virtue whereby we tend toward God. In this purification, souls overcome an excessive desire for temporal goods, a too great confidence in themselves, gaining a true view of our frailty. God never permits souls to be tempted beyond their strength, but at this stage, souls are

---

[420] Garrigou-Lagrange, *The Three Ages of the Interior Life*, vol. 2, p. 403.

[421] Sensible devotion means an inordinate desire for feeling good about praying, like only going to Mass if it feels good.

given the greatest trials. God removes Himself sensibly so these souls hope against all hope. They focus on reparation and repeat David's words: "Thy face, O Lord, will I still seek."[422] "But at the same time, these souls should have no delusions; but should realize that they will not attain victory except by passing through Calvary."[423] Souls recognize the value of total abandonment to the divine will and the duty of the present moment. This means not to worry about the past or the future because there is nothing we can do about it. The devil tries to bring these souls to despair by tempting them with an inordinate concern for the past or the future. It is necessary, then, to bind the demons away in the name of Jesus and to live to be a saint now, because God is the eternal *now*. At the end of this trial, hope is no longer mingled with self-love.

Charity is greatly perfected in the passive purification. Trials resemble purgatory. Charity is transformed into loving God only for Himself, because He loved us first and He wants us to participate in His infinite life. Charity loves God for Himself and is purified of loving the consolations of God. When God takes away His consolations for months or years, He becomes more intimately present in the soul. Souls here see God is infinitely good in Himself. At this stage, souls see clearly this motive of charity in all its elevation, like a star of first magnitude in the night of the spirit.

We read, in fact, toward the end of the life of Saint Thérèse of the Child of Jesus and of the Holy Face:

> He then allowed my soul to be invaded by the thickest darkness, and the thought of heaven, which had been so

[422] Ps. 26:8.

[423] Fr. Gabriel of St. Mary Magdalen, O.C.D., *Divine Intimacy*, no. 338.

> sweet to me since my early childhood, became for me a subject for struggle and torment. . . . I wish I could express what I feel, but it is impossible. One must have passed through this dark tunnel to understand my obscurity. . . . When weary of the surrounding darkness, I wish to rest my heart by the fortifying memory of a future and eternal life, [but] my torment redoubles. . . .
>
> Knowing that it is cowardly to fight a duel, I turn my back on my adversary without ever looking at him in the face, then I run to Jesus and tell Him that I am ready to shed every drop of my blood to acknowledge that there is a heaven.

What are the sufferings in this purification? Persons who we thought were our friends desert us, few think well of us, but many hate us, and severe bodily infirmity comes. This royal road of suffering is the way to heaven. It is *Ad lucem per crucem*, "to the light through the cross."

Now, turn to the prayers to be recited during the *unitive* way and the Chaplet of the Holy Face (p. 159, 20).

# Day 27

## The Holy Face and Our Lady of Seven Dolors

"Call me not Noemi, (that is, beautiful,) but call me Mara, (that is, bitter,) for the Almighty hath quite filled me with bitterness."[424]

---

[424] Ruth 1:20. The Latin *amaram* means "bitterness." Saint Louis de Montfort compares Mary to a sea, from the Latin *mare*.

Jesus looks upon Mary with His Holy Face, and Mary looks at His and cannot recognize His features. Each look renews the bitterness of the Sacred Heart and the Immaculate Heart. As this was the moment of the greatest triumph of Christ our King, this was the moment of Mary's greatest virtue.

Jesus was placed upon the cross, placed among criminals, mocked and maltreated by His people, and steeped in outrages by menials and executioners. Mary, what do you see when you look at His Holy Face? Is it the Face you adored in the stable of Bethlehem? Or the Face in the Temple when held by the holy old man and Anna? Behold His Face now upon the cross.

Then Jesus rests His eyes upon Saint John and opens His lips, "Woman, behold thy son. After that, he saith to the disciple: Behold thy mother."[425] At that moment, Mary receives guilty humanity. Oh, how we need to become like Saint John, the contemplative. He had the deepest prayer life and was the only one of the apostles to brave the cross. He was thus united inseparably to the august Mother, to follow her steps, to live with her, and to love and suffer with her.

My dear Jesus upon the cross, look too upon me and ask the Blessed Virgin Mary and Saint John to intercede for me so that I may enjoy the spiritual age of the perfect and be united with Thee. Help me to have a constant conversation with heaven and soar like the eagle toward the sun, scrutinizing the depths of the horizon. Give me the grace of prolonged spiritual communion and an ardent love of Thy divine liturgies. May I receive the Beatific Vision immediately after death without having to pass purgatory, which is the secret of the saints.

---

[425] John 19:26–27.

## The Spiritual Age of the Perfect, Their Union with God and Spiritual Childhood

The painful passive purification is like the crucifixion and passion of Jesus. Afterwards, it is the Resurrection. The apostles experienced their passion after Jesus left in His ascension, but their resurrection was at Pentecost, where they were strengthened to preach the Gospel, even to the point of their blood.

After the third conversion, the perfect know God almost continually, not just at Mass, Divine Office, or prayer, but throughout the day, even amidst external occupations.

The egoist, having never gone through the first purification, enjoys having constant conversation with himself, which is endless, sterile, and vain. But souls in this last stage continually talk to God about His glory and the salvation of souls. They have progressed from seeing God in sensible things, as do beginners. They have arrived at the stage of proficient, who, as in a mirror, contemplates God in the mysteries of the life of Christ. They finally reach the summit of the perfect, contemplating God and His goodness in itself.

Souls in union have moved from linear prayer, like the lark who repeatedly flies from nest to ground, and have progressed to circular prayer, like the eagle that flies toward the sun in spirals, scrutinizing the depths of the horizon, as was said above.[426] The perfect contemplates events as from the summit of a mountain, seeing things on the plains below. This is similar to God, who sees events at once, looking down from the peak of eternity, beholding all of time at a glance.

---

[426] Garrigou-Lagrange, *The Three Ages of the Interior Life*, vol. 2, p. 428.

Unitives see themselves always in relationship to God and so never get discouraged by their sins but become humbler through them. They consider themselves wicked servants of God but are used by Him to do great things. They see others greater than themselves due to the thought of their hidden faults and others' hidden virtues. "These souls feel a great interior joy when persecuted . . . they conceive for them a particular affection."[427]

How do they love God with their whole mind? They only desire to adhere to Him by prolonged spiritual communions. They desire heaven and attend the Divine Liturgies less for themselves, but to render eternally the glory due to God.

How does the Blessed Trinity dwell in perfect souls? The perfect become like walking, living tabernacles. The more perfect they are, the more noticeable is this presence to their neighbor. Close union is not extraordinary but ordinary for each of the baptized, but it is very rare in our times because of a lack of generosity. The perfect are like the disciples on the road to Emmaus, whose hearts were burning within them. In this state, God inspires the most profound, magnanimous acts that souls would not have been able to do on their own.

What are the signs of the indwelling, according to Saint Thomas in the *Summa Contra Gentiles*?

1. Good conscience—not aware of having committed mortal sin.[428]
2. Joy in hearing the word of God—they want to be preached to of the traditional things of faith.

---

[427] Tanquerey, Very Rev. Adolphe, *The Spiritual Life*, no. 1475.

[428] Not to be confused with the under catechized who do not know that missing Mass on Sunday is grave matter for mortal sin, for example.

3. Relish of divine wisdom—willing to read the Gospel privately.[429]
4. Converse intimately with God—"our conversation is in heaven."[430]
5. Rejoicing in God—fully consenting to His will in every adversity.
6. Liberty of the children of God—not like slaves, but like free creatures.
7. Indwelling of the Blessed Trinity—Ven. Leo DuPont had a sign in his parlor: "Once business is done, depart unless only the things of God are spoken of."

It has been witnessed by the author that souls who make a total consecration to the Holy Face of Jesus are led to the upper mansions in the kingdom. A sign that one has arrived, or has the generosity to be on his way, is that he has read to this point. But it is one thing to know from reading. It is necessary to live it out completely. When that happens, that is a personal Pentecost.

How is spiritual childhood part of the perfect life? The soul is not childish but childlike. A child is spontaneous, he does not pose, and he says what is on his mind. These are the qualities of a toddler. A child of God is like the toddler, minus all the defects. He recognizes that without God's grace, he is nothing. His faith is devoid of human respect. He looks into the Holy Face like a child looks into the face of his father. He is completely abandoned to Providence and is faithful to the duty in

[429] And accept the interpretation from the Church's tradition.
[430] Phil. 3:20.

his state at each moment. He loves his Father in trial as in times of joy. They have such courage in adversity, and the virtue and gift of fortitude are united, which leads to transforming union that is seen in the saints.

"Perfection consists in taking the place of Mary and doing the work of Martha at one and the same time."[431] The whole Rosary,[432] prayed daily, can assist toward perfection because it brings humility and a desire for loving contemplation, the fruit of constant prayer.

Now, turn to the prayers to be recited during the *unitive* way and the Chaplet of the Holy Face (p. 159, 20).

## Day 28

### The Last Words which Fell from the Lips of the Holy Face

It is now the end of the sorrowful drama. Nature gives signs of mourning, uniting herself to the friends of Jesus. Darkness covers the whole earth. The sun is obscured, making three hours of darkness. His lips are saturated with bitterness, He sees that nothing can be added to His suffering. He utters His last cry: *Consummatum est.*[433] The cry tears from top to bottom[434] the veil in the Temple; the earth trembles. "Father," He says, "into

[431] Tanquerey, Very Rev. Adolphe, *The Spiritual Life*, no. 1478.
[432] Before modern times, the whole Rosary was fifteen decades, 150 Ave Marias, which is comparable to the Psalms, which are also 150.
[433] See John 19:30.
[434] A miracle; as the veil was very tall, was torn at an instant and too far for someone to reach it.

Thy hands I commend My spirit."[435] Behold the Holy Face of Jesus: first It breaths forth from His afflicted Heart a deep sigh. Then It bows down Its head in token of Its obedience. And finally, offering up the death for the salvation of men, at length, through the violence of pain, expires.[436]

"Father, forgive them, for they know not what they do. This day thou shalt be with me in paradise." Even to the end of bitter suffering, a glance of the Holy Face looks upon enemies and forgives sinners. He gives us Mary from the summit of His victory. He thus thirsts for souls and suffering.

My Lord Jesus Christ, make me like unto Thee crucified. I beg for discernment from the Holy Ghost, so that I may consider devotion to Mary in the unitive way. Communicate to me a heroic degree of virtues, that I may give Thee ever more glory and snatch souls from falling into hell like snowflakes.

## The Heroic Degree of the Virtues in General

Dear soul, consider the heroic degree of the virtues which Pope Benedict XIV required the Church to discern for beatification of the servants of God. Heroic virtue begins in the illuminative way, it is matured in the third conversion of passive purification, and reaches its zenith in the unitive way. When the soul emerges in the preceding dark tunnels to the unitive way, the soul joins the perfect.

---

[435] Luke 23:46. The "seven last words" are translated by eight in the English, but seven in the Latin: *Pater, in manus tuas commendo spiritum meam.*

[436] Liguori, St. Alphonsus, *The Passion and Death of Jesus Christ*, pp. 127–128.

What are distinctive marks of heroic virtue? Saint Thomas explains that if a courageous man fears what he should fear, it is a virtue; otherwise, he would sin in temerity. "But if he no longer fears anything, because he relies on the help of God, then it is a superhuman or divine virtue."[437] Another sign is that he lives the beatitudes in totality.

Virtue is first rooted in social virtues, then perfecting virtues, and last, those of the purified soul. The traditional teaching of heroic virtues is summed up by Pope Benedict XIV:

1. The matter or object should be difficult, above the common strength of man.
2. The acts should be accomplished promptly, easily.
3. They should be performed with holy joy.
4. They should be accomplished quite frequently.[438]

Suffering must be involved, but heroic charity surmounts it. The joy of suffering for Christ increases while suffering. Martyrdom is the standard sign. This mirrors the passion of Christ.

Confessors are quick to pardon injuries. For example, consider Father Henry Mary Boudon.[439] When his bishop received a calumnious letter regarding him, he was forbidden to celebrate Mass and hear confession. On receipt of the penalty, he immediately threw himself at the foot of the crucifix and thanked God for this grace of which he thought himself unworthy.[440]

---

[437] Commentary on Matt. v, lect. I.

[438] *De servorum Dei beatificatione*, Bk. III, ch. 21.

[439] Archdeacon of Evreux, counselor to many bishops in France, and author of many excellent books.

[440] Garrigou-Lagrange, *The Three Ages of the Interior Life*, vol. 2, p. 444.

Souls in this age of the spiritual life have received not only acquired virtues and infused virtues but the perfection of the gifts in their nature, all of which work at the service of charity. Heroic fraternal charity is a perfect love because one can live among the wicked without being harsh or contentious, without being influenced by them, but rather doing them good and praying for them.[441]

How are these virtues connected? The great test is practicing all the virtues simultaneously. Why? Each one's temperament is determined in one direction. Melancholics find prayer easy but public speaking difficult. Souls here overcome their natural defects. The summit of perfection is achieved by climbing different slopes because God, Who is pleased to vary His gifts and adapt them to the different temperaments and characters, does not confine His action within set forms; and so when reading the mystics, one finds very different forms of contemplation.[442] If all the virtues are annexed, there are about forty. It follows that a virtue exists in the heroic degree only if the others exist in proportionate degree.[443]

The opposite may help. Although pagans have a love for country, a part of piety, they almost always lack some of the forty other virtues. The highest sign is one who prays for his executioners and enemies like, Jesus did. False martyrs endure their torments through pride and obstinacy in error; whereas, true martyrs pray for their executioners. Extreme circumstances give extreme grace. For example, St. Simeon, second bishop in Jerusalem (after St. James was martyred), was crucified at the

---

441 Fr. Gabriel of St. Mary Magdalen, O.C.D., *Divine Intimacy*, no. 70.
442 Tanquerey, Very Rev. Adolphe, *The Spiritual Life*, no. 1418.
443 Garrigou-Lagrange, p. 446.

age of 120 and preached to his people from the cross during his passion.

What is heroic and contemplative faith? They are the visible fruit of contemplation in souls who are in almost constant conversation with God.

What kind of firmness is heroic? Despite demonic temptation, it is a realization of how infinite justice and infinite mercy are harmonized. The devil tells souls that God's justice is excessively rigorous and His mercy is arbitrary. But having passed through the tunnel, they now see past that lie, rise above the temptation, and receive a divine grace—namely, that the darkness from these mysteries comes from a light too bright for weak eyes of the spirit.[444] They are firm even in the most minute details of doctrine or tradition proposed by the Church. Their faith is great, like Abraham, who was willing to sacrifice Isaac. "St. Catherine was told by Jesus to look at His passion from a spiritual point of view: 'Daughter embrace the Cross and for My sake look on all sweet things as bitter, and all bitter things as sweet, and so be certain that you will always be strong.'"[445] The heroic quickly perceive errors that are small in appearance. Saint Vincent de Paul was able to see the errors of Jansenism, which were opposed to the divine mercy and keeping the faithful from Communion. After alerting Rome, he helped many souls along the right way. This promptness, though, causes the servants of God much suffering. They have a great zeal for propagating the faith, not by a bitter zeal, but by fervent and almost continual prayer, which should be the soul of the apostolate.[446]

---

[444] Garrigou-Lagrange, p. 451.

[445] Forbes, *St. Catherine of Siena*, p. 12.

[446] Garrigou-Lagrange, p. 453.

What kind of penetration do heroic souls have? Their perfect faith helps them see everything in the light of God, Scripture, and the Church. God the Father remarked in Saint Catherine's *Dialogue*: "Those who belong to the third state . . . deem themselves worthy of the troubles and stumbling blocks caused them by the world, and of the privation of their own consolation, and indeed of whatever circumstance happens to them. . . . They have known and tasted in the light of my eternal will, which wishes naught else but your good and gives and permits these troubles in order that you should be sanctified by Me."[447]

Sometimes, the faith illumines the face of the saints. When a group waited in ambush to kill Saint Dominic, his face shone with a celestial ray, and it convinced the murderers to forego the kill. Holy Face of Jesus, radiant for all eternity, pray for us!

Now, turn to the prayers to be recited during the *unitive* way and the Chaplet of the Holy Face (p. 159, 20).

## Day 29

### The Holy Face Washed and Perfumed by Mary

The shades of death have quitted the lips and closed the eyes of our Redeemer, but faith allows us to behold the uncreated light which angels and saints adore.

Mary washes His feet, which walked the dusty roads teaching us the way of salvation, and His sacred hands, which lifted up the holy chalice of His Precious Blood. But Our Lady was attracted to one object of Him in a singular way: His Holy Face.

---

[447] Catherine of Siena, *The Dialogue*, ch. 99.

It was through His lips that He uttered secret consolations to her, but which are now silent.

May my eyes and lips close to the vanities of the world, and may my soul tend to God, the object of eternal beatitude.

O Jesus, Lord of the living, when every human help disappears amidst calumnies and rebuffs, may I abandon myself into Thy arms as Thou didst run into the arms of Our Lady of Perpetual Help when the angels carried the cross and instruments of Thy passion. Blessed Virgin, it is a sign of predestination for souls to recommend themselves to thee. Please intercede for me that I may place all my hope in Jesus.

## Heroic Hope, Abandonment, and Charity

Weak hope is still susceptible to the fluctuations of presumption and discouragement. The devil tries to tempt these souls by dragging them one way and then another. But heroic hope, tending toward God, has an invincible firmness, trusting abandonment, and unwavering fidelity to duty.

The Lord lets every human help disappear. This usually results in calumnies and rebuffs, often also with physical suffering. Heroic hope responds by observing a clearer view of one's wretchedness and by overcoming depression inherent in chronic illness. The soul here hopes against human hope, as Saint Paul comments on the hope of Abraham and his sacrifice of Isaac.

Although hope grows tenfold and more, the Council of Trent says that we cannot be certain that we are in the state of grace unless it is revealed to us. Remember the story above about Saint Joan of Arc's response to her persecutors. Hope grows heroically if we allow God to crush us in order for us to grow.

How does abandonment look at this state? Heroic hope increases by trusting abandonment to Providence and the omnipotent goodness of God. God makes the soul come to the highest ramparts of a fortress, from which it sees the nothingness of things here below.[448] It is an understanding that nothing escapes Providence; at every moment, God wills goodness in creation. It rests ever more on the infinite merits of our Redeemer. It tastes Providence by the gift of wisdom, which shows all things in God, and this taste is far superior to sensible consolation. The soul does not want to have any will of its own; it would even wish to forgo the possession of its free will, were that possible.[449] In the saints, in the proportion that charity grows, the fear of suffering diminishes.

What does heroic charity look like? Charity makes us love God for Himself and our neighbor in God. Heroic charity means the soul wishes His holy will in the greatest difficulties and the salvation of souls. It loves God without consolation, in spite of aridity, mourning because it loves the God of all consolations Himself, who he cannot presently have. The soul wishes to be alone with God, especially in front of the Blessed Sacrament. It receives lovingly every painful occurrence as coming from God's positive or permissive will, like David who bore the insults of Semei.[450] In all trials, the saints say, "It is as God wishes." "The greatest sign of heroic charity toward God, is an insatiable thirst for suffering because if He wishes them to

[448] Tanquerey, Very Rev. Adolphe, *The Spiritual Life*, no. 1462.
[449] Tanquerey, Very Rev. Adolphe, *The Spiritual Life*, no. 1462.
[450] Kgs. (2 Sam.) 16:10.

suffer, they are content."[451] Souls that work on patience and abandonment to God's will are led to this love.

When souls are tempted to envy or discord, heroic charity shines when they dominate the temptation by acting in charity. In the midst of great difficulties, these souls respond by assuming good will in the other, speaking well of him, and being quick to pardon.

Heroic love of neighbor was exemplified in the ransom orders.[452] They traded places with those enslaved in order to free them. Great missionaries also exemplified zeal for souls, like Saint Francis Xavier and Saint Francis de Sales.[453] Saints are attractive because the more united they are to God, the more they draw others to Him.

Now, turn to the prayers to be recited during the *unitive* way and the Chaplet of the Holy Face (p. 159, 20).

## Day 30

### The Holy Face of the Sepulcher

After having been kissed by Mary and wrapped by the Magdalen, the Holy Face disappears in the sepulcher. The shroud of Turin, like the veil of Veronica, will have the lineaments of Jesus.

---

[451] Tanquerey, Very Rev. Adolphe, *The Spiritual Life*, no. 1475.

[452] Members of the Trinitarians or Mercedarians (a few of the ransom orders) would go to the slaves of Muslims and "ransom" them by giving themselves up in return for the freedom of the captive.

[453] The former baptized between one and two million pagans. The latter reverted 72,000 fallen away Catholics in four years.

It was custom for Jews to have their beloved deceased buried with a full linen covering the body before placing it in a cavity of rock. Joseph of Arimathea purchased this sepulcher for Jesus, who had no place to lay His head. In addition to this linen covering, the shroud, the friends of the Archconfraternity of the Holy Face especially venerate the impression left on the veil of Veronica, the Holy Face of Jesus, as the chief object of the Passion and of reparation. But meditating on the Holy Shroud as object of the death is reserved for this chapter.

History shows the shroud passed from Nicodemus to Saint James, to Saint Simeon,[454] to the crusaders, and finally to its current location, Turin, in the House of Savoy.

In the secret design of God, the image of Our Lord's shroud was impressed with signs of the thorns and blows. He suffered so much for me, why cannot I suffer for love of the crucified and Mary to find the deepest union with God? I must renounce all desire to attract notice, to be honored, sought after, and loved. I do well to pray with the apostles of devotion to the Holy Face: Sister Marie de Saint-Pierre, the author of the Litanies of the Holy Face, and the venerable M. DuPont, who often recited these prayers to be more united to Jesus Christ crucified and to join the profound union of the Blessed Virgin Mary.

Dear Holy Ghost, who didst say, "A man is known by his look and a wise man . . . is known by his countenance,"[455] descend upon me with an abundance of the Holy Gifts. By them, may God the Father draw me to Himself in an exponential degree, so that my contemplation of the Holy Face of Jesus will be ever communicated to my face the fire of His infinite love.

---

[454] As mentioned above, St. Simeon was the second bishop of Jerusalem, ended his life at age 120, preaching to his flock from a cross.

[455] Ecclus. 19:26.

## Heroic Degree of Christian Moral Virtues and Jesus Crucified

Humility drives out inordinate love of self, considers all greater than oneself in order to abase oneself before the majesty of God. Those who live heroic humility are especially humble toward those who make them suffer. It led Saint Peter to desire to be crucified upside down. The humble man here lets his modesty be known to the world by his calm, humble countenance. He is little inclined to laughter and possesses an unaffected bearing which shows his love of contemplation and his uninterrupted conversation with God.[456]

Heroic fortitude endures sorrows without murmuring and endures trials for a long time, the fruit of longanimity. He lives with magnanimity, the lofty practice of the virtues. Heroic fortitude is especially a witness of martyrdom. Patience and magnanimity are practiced when something heroic is to be accomplished.

Heroic prudence required the soul to always act as a child of God in perfect dependence on Him. Souls here are apt to see the true good to be done and firmly direct the other virtues to accomplish this in a good and holy manner. This virtue is absolutely necessary in order for souls to arrive at deep union with God. God purifies souls who place too much trust in their own prudence with rebuffs, lack of memory, failures, and bad health. Heroic prudence is accompanied with the gift of counsel in an eminent degree. The author has seen this gift of counsel exemplified in a nun who introduced him to the Holy Face devotion.

Heroic justice allows union with God because these souls are irreproachable in their dealing with others. They practice

[456] Garrigou-Lagrange, *The Three Ages of the Interior Life*, vol. 2, p. 474.

justice heroically because they know that God will overthrow their enemies.[457] Our Lord said one must love Him more than family members. A heroic example is when a magistrate has to decide against his grievously guilty son.

What does love of Jesus Crucified and of Mary in the unitive way look like? They must have a love of the humanity of Jesus Christ and not just His divinity. Otherwise, as Saint Teresa says, "the devil might end by robbing us of our devotion to the Most Blessed Sacrament." All the saints lived to the end of their lives with devotion to the Sacred Humanity. Our Father communicates the riches of His Son, His intellect, His will, and His sensibility. The soul in union with Him sees more clearly the victory of Christ won by the cross and the glory and majesty of His triumph over the kingdom of Satan. Souls have a yearning for daily Mass and Communion because they see the infinite value in it. Souls with true devotion, when they receive Holy Communion, accelerate their union noticeably. They see the excellence of the devotion of Mary and her unique union. "Mary is, at the same time the model of both contemplative and apostolic souls. Furthermore, by combining in herself the highest contemplative life with the highest apostolic life, she teaches that contemplation and the apostolate far from being opposed to each other, complement, support and maintain each other."[458]

Now, turn to the prayers to be recited during the *unitive* way and the Chaplet of the Holy Face (p. 159, 20).

---

[457] See Ecclus. 4:33–36.

[458] Fr. Gabriel of St. Mary Magdalen, O.C.D., *Divine Intimacy*, no. 84.

# Day 31

## The Holy Face after the Resurrection

In fulfillment of the types in the Old Testament, Jesus Himself, after lying in the grave for three days, rose from the dead. In private revelation, Jesus appears to the Blessed Virgin Mary at three o'clock on Easter morning.[459] He appeared later to Mary Magdalen and then to the apostles. Although His adorable Face was shining with glory and beauty, their eyes were not dazzled by Its splendor. Many evil men and blasphemers were never to see the resurrected Jesus, but only those who were friends of Christ, those who believed in the Way. The Resurrection was the time of His triumph, but it was not the hour of celestial glory. This would be revealed at the Ascension.

The rays emitting from His five glorious wounds were veiled so as not to blind the disciples. His Face still had traces of scars from the crown of thorns and other blows, but they were shown as such, fitting for His resurrected body. The lips were no longer swollen, but traces of the blows left by the executioners remained.

My Jesus, change me to be open to the wisdom Thou bestowed on Thy disciples. Cast Thine eyes, illuminated by the glory of the Resurrection, upon my soul, formerly disfigured by iniquity. Grant me the grace of contemplating Thy Holy Face in its fullness so that I may live the apostolic life in my state perfectly and pour myself out as Thou shed Thy blood: in total reparation for blasphemy and profanations of Sundays.

---

[459] Agreda, *Mystical City of God*, vol. 3, p. 727.

## Perfect Apostolic Life, Contemplation, and Reparation

Ven. Leo DuPont led a perfect apostolic life, assisting Sr. Marie de St. Pierre as an apostle of the Holy Face. After he was done conducting work as a lawyer, he generously spent his time promoting the messages of Jesus given to Sister. He did this by healing over six thousand people, with the oil burning day and night in front of his relic of the veil of Veronica. He was a model for the laity.

Those in the clerical state or missionaries in the religious life live the perfect apostolic life when the fullness of contemplation proceeds to teaching and preaching. Those in the wholly contemplative life live their state perfectly by constant conversion of life, tending toward contemplation/union as an end in itself, but not without a hidden apostolic fruitfulness.

Heroic zeal for souls is part of the perfect apostolic life: "The Venerable Father Louis la Nuza was seen in heaven sitting on a lofty throne at the foot of which were seated all the souls that he had converted."[460]

The eminent source of the apostolic life comes from knowing Christ and imitating Him and His apostles. Saint Peter spoke with the authority of the Holy Ghost after Pentecost: "You by the hands of wicked men have crucified and slain. Whom God hath raised up."[461] The preaching that proceeds from the fullness of contemplation overflows also in the epistles of Saint Paul.

The soul of the apostolate requires exact observance in external practice of the divine liturgies, study, and penance,

---

[460] Liguori, St. Alphonsus, *The Dignities and Duties of the Priesthood*, p. 175.
[461] Acts 2:23.

but contemplation is the fire that brings conversions. Souls who are simply in the presence of these saints and hear the preaching of these great apostolic men are converted by the fire of the Holy Ghost. Union with God must be the source of every apostolate, but today, sadly, it seems almost non-existent. Why? "Love of neighbor," some say, "is superior to love of God; this would constitute heresy that would overthrow the very order of charity."[462] This is one among many of the errors of modernism. But devotion to Mary can help us avoid this modern error. "The apostle cannot claim to have a sufficient devotion to Our Lady if his confidence in her is almost entirely external. Like her Son *intuetur cor*, she only looks at our hearts, and judges us to be her true children only by the power with which our love corresponds to hers."[463]

Every good thing in the Church starts with the interior life. Jesus willed contemplation and union with God, not as subordinated to action, but as fructifying the apostolate *and good and necessary as an end in itself.* A great spirit of faith is a sign of an ardent love of God and souls. How does one arrive at this lofty state? One must hunger to grow in liturgical and mental prayer. Union with God is chiefly found in the celebration of the Holy *Sacrifice* of the Mass, which is the summit of our faith. What happens in the sanctuary, whether there is reverence or irreverence, determines what happens in the world.

What is the condition for a fruitful apostolate? Apostles cannot save souls by preaching without suffering for them. Great returns cannot be expected unless there are obstacles, calumnies, insults, and suffering. But this is when generosity

---

[462] Garrigou-Lagrange, *The Three Ages of the Interior Life*, vol. 2, p. 491.
[463] Fr. Chautard, *Soul of the Apostolate*, p. 283.

is paramount, because Jesus has chosen our crosses for us and offers them to us as the material of the crowns and thrones He is preparing for us and as a test of our virtue and fidelity in His service. In a word, we do well to desire what sufferings with which God wishes to visit us, nothing less, nothing more.

How does a life of reparation manifest itself? It must be a life of the cross. Jesus chiefly saved the world not by sermons but by the cross. A life of reparation means living as a victim for God. Of the four ends of sacrifice—petition, thanksgiving, adoration, and reparation[464]—it seems, first, that reparation is typically the least practiced. When Christians were baptized, the life of Christ was placed in them. Jesus gave Sr. Marie de St. Pierre His Holy Face to make reparation.[465]

Since reparation is part of the life of Christ, it cannot be ignored. The Christian should learn the life of reparation from the priest. The priest should be a crucified man. The priest should be consumed. He should live as if he were to die a martyr today.

Saint Alphonsus Liguori is a great example. When he was eighty years of age, he was already purified, and his great trials in the end were chiefly reparation for the sanctification of sinners. They were not to be confused with passive purification of the senses, found in the second conversion.

The Blessed Virgin Mary had a heavy cross to carry, but her seven sorrows and the rest of her trials allowed her to penetrate the mystery of the altar far more than did the apostle Saint John when he celebrated the Mass in her presence and gave her Holy Communion. Her reparation at Mass rendered the apostolate of the Twelve very fruitful.

---

[464] Sometimes, satisfaction or atonement is used for reparation.

[465] See Scallan, *The Golden Arrow*, p. 158.

Our Lady has given to some souls a vision of a crown of glory or a crown of thorns. They are free to choose between the two. Some, after having chosen the easier crown, were convinced by Our Lady to choose the thorns instead. Those who chose the configuration to Christ crucified by the life of reparation prepare themselves for the immediate prelude to eternal life. Saint Paul of the Cross received a signal grace from the Blessed Virgin Mary, a gold ring which represented the instruments of the Passion.

Our Lord revealed to Sr. Marie de St. Pierre in 1847: "I have already told you that I hold you in my hands as an arrow. I now want to hurl this arrow against my enemies. To arm you for the battle ahead, I give you the weapons of My Passion, that is My Cross which these enemies dread, and also the other instruments of my tortures. Go forward to meet these foes with the artlessness of a child, and the bravery of a courageous soldier. Receive for this mission the benediction of the Father, of the Son, and of the Holy Ghost."[466]

Now, turn to the prayers to be recited during the *unitive* way and the Chaplet of the Holy Face (p. 159, 20).

# Day 32

## The Holy Face and the Eucharist

Sr. Marie de St. Pierre wrote the Litany of the Holy Face, which includes: "Oh adorable Face, hidden in the Eucharist, have pity on us." Saint Thomas affirms that the Holy Face of Jesus possesses the faculty of seeing with the eyes of the body in the

[466] Scanlan, *The Golden Arrow*, p. 203.

Holy Eucharist.[467] His body, blood, soul, and divinity are present in the Holy Eucharist, so His Sacred Body contains also the Holy Face. "It was the same body bruised for our crimes, the same heart, which was transpierced on the cross, the same Holy Face scarred in the praetorian, and to which was offered the gall and drink."[468]

Cardinal Franzelin explains that Our Lord, in the Holy Eucharist, has the use of His external senses. Moses asked to see the Face of God but was denied because he would not live after seeing It. But we are allowed to see the Face of Jesus without dying, who under the species of the Body, He does not unveil the splendor of His glories.

O my soul, come before the presence of the Holy Face, veiled underneath bread and wine, and spend sufficient time there, so that He may gaze upon your soul and make the fire of His love penetrate it. Come to vent your feelings and speak heart to heart with this most devoted of friends.

## *Prayer of Ven. Leo DuPont*

O Savior Jesus! At the sight of Thy most Holy Face disfigured by suffering, at the sight of Thy Sacred Heart so full of love, I exclaim with St. Augustine—"Lord Jesus, imprint upon my heart Thy sacred wounds, that I may read therein both Thy sorrow and Thy love—Thy sorrow, that for Thy sake I may suffer all grief; Thy love, that for Thy sake I may despise all other love."

---

[467] Disp. III, Sub. IV, 3.

[468] Garrigou-Lagrange, *The Three Ages of the Interior Life*, vol. 2, p. 498.

## The Influence of the Holy Ghost in the Perfect Soul and Ecstatic Union

The hierarchy of gifts from God are, from lowest to greatest:

1. Natural gifts (i.e., beauty),
2. Sanctifying grace—created gift, and
3. the Holy Ghost—uncreated gift par excellence.

Jesus stated, "If thou didst know the gift of God"![469] The third divine person proceeds eternally from the mutual love of the Father and the Son. After Jesus gave us the Holy Eucharist, His precious blood, and all the sacraments, He gave us the Holy Ghost at Pentecost. The apostles, after receiving the Holy Ghost, were transformed and led by the Holy Ghost even to martyrdom.

The Holy Ghost is the Comforter. A help in suffering is to think about how the martyrs suffered their very painful tortures. The Holy Ghost strengthened them. He comforts us in the sorrows and anxieties of life. The Holy Ghost strengthens, preserves, and increases the gift of sanctifying grace in souls, like the fountain of water springing up into everlasting life, as Jesus spoke to the Samaritan woman.

The Holy Ghost dwells in a light too bright for us, but He strengthens our faith and makes suffering sweet when we surrender to it. "All Three Persons here communicate themselves to [the soul] and speak to her and make her understand all those words in the Gospel where Our Lord said that He, and the Father and the Holy Ghost would come and dwell with the

---

[469] John 4:10.

soul that loves Him and keeps His commandments."[470] Our love is small, but when the Holy Ghost dwells within and loves the Father and the Son, there is a certain quality of loving God as He loves Himself. The *Imitation* speaks, "The noble love of Jesus inspires us to do great things, and exciteth us always to desire that which is the more perfect. . . . Like a vivid flame and a burning torch, it mounteth upward and securely passes through all."[471]

Saint Catherine of Siena said these words from Jesus, "In perfect souls the Holy Ghost weeps tears of fire."[472] This gift of tears happens at the sight of sin and the thought of souls falling into hell, like snowflakes. "These spiritual tears often obtain the remission of great sins."[473]

Spending ample time with the Holy Face of Jesus before the Blessed Sacrament is a great way to be more receptive to the Holy Ghost, who communicates the love of the cross and a share in suffering according to Providence. Peace, joy, and strength are given especially to those who love consecration to the Holy Ghost and consecration to the Holy Face of Jesus. The Blessed Virgin Mary expedites the preparation of perfect souls to receive the Holy Ghost in mystical union, which is normally the seed of the Beatific Vision, the unveiling of the Face of God.

## Arid Mystical Union

Arid mystical union is a painful union with the Holy Ghost that corresponds to the night of the spirit. It is a terrible crucible

---

[470] St. Teresa of Avila, *Interior Castle*, 7th Mansion C. I.

[471] Thomas à Kempis, *The Imitation of Christ*, Bk. III, ch. 5, passion.

[472] Catherine of Siena, *Dialogue*, ch. 91.

[473] Garrigou-Lagrange, *The Three Ages of the Interior Life*, vol. 2, p. 516.

where friends sometimes change into enemies; confessors do not know how to help, as they perceive the soul as being punished for sin; and temptations strongly suggest that God has rejected the soul. But suffering all this well makes the soul realize that this test is required to prove love of God. The Comforter assures the soul that the evil spirits can do no more harm than God permits. In this trial, the soul suffers purification, like one going through purgatory.[474]

## Ecstatic Union

Ecstatic union can precede, accompany, or follow the fires of mystical union, can express itself exteriorly, and is described thus: It can consist of fainting spells, which produce hurt but then delight, raptures where the soul seems to be taken by an eagle, and flight of the spirit where it seems to be in another region quite different from this world.[475] It strengthens the body and gives one the ability, for example, to kneel longer than physically possible. The soul is absorbed in God and loses its use of the senses. The will is freely moved vehemently, as the soul moves its activity into its higher part.[476] Ecstasy can last from a few moments up to about four days.

Obedience is easily practiced in ecstatics. When Saint Padre Pio was in ecstasy, he would not respond to conversation unless it was a superior who commanded under obedience. It is not to be confused with diabolical ecstasy or a sort of obsession, because the soul in that case gives way to unseemly contortions

[474] Teresa of Avila, *The Interior Castle*, 6th Mansion, ch. 11.

[475] Tanquerey, Very Rev. Adolphe, *The Spiritual Life*, no. 1466.

[476] Garrigou-Lagrange, p. 523.

and utters incoherent words. Ecstasy is like a dress rehearsal before more continual union. This continual union is called transforming union or spiritual marriage. Saint Thomas says that ecstasy is less than rapture because ecstasy is a going out of oneself, but rapture denotes a certain violence in addition.[477]

What are the effects of ecstatic union? The soul sees a great clearness in the Lord's passion and the Seven Dolors of Mary and possesses a great holiness of life. After ecstatic union, God gives a painful suffering of the will, in which the soul sees itself deprived of all joy, becoming convinced that this state will last forever.[478] Saint Teresa says, "The heart receives, it knows not how or whence, a blow as from a fiery dart."[479] This stage before continual union does not last more than three or four hours, because if it went longer, the weakness of nature could not endure it, save a miracle. Sometimes, the wounds of the stigmata are left behind.

Now, turn to the prayers to be recited during the *unitive* way and the Chaplet of the Holy Face (p. 159, 20).

## Day 33

### The Holy Face on the Last Day

"Strive to enter by the narrow gate; for many I say to you, shall seek to enter, and shall not be able."[480] Dear soul, to live by faith in these words will prove a happy last day, for after the resurrection of the body and the separation of the good from the

[477] *Summa Theologica* II–II, q. 175.

[478] Garrigou-Lagrange, p. 526.

[479] Teresa of Avila, *The Interior Castle*, 6th Mansion, ch. 11, passion.

[480] Luke 13:24.

wicked, only those who lived the maxims of the Gospel will rejoice on this terrible day.

The standard of the Sovereign Judge, the sign of the Son of Man, the cross,[481] will be seen appearing in the air. Jesus will be borne by Cherubim, surrounded by a thousand million angels who form His court. "With a single glance, He reads the book of consciences."[482]

The Holy Face will appear terrible before the wicked. They treated the prophets and Jesus Himself worse than their least slaves. They will look for mercy, but the time for mercy has passed. He will launch forth one of those terrible glances of which David said, "He looketh upon the earth and maketh it tremble; He toucheth the mountains, and they smoke."[483]

They will wish to hide in the depths of the earth, but each is to receive his due in the time of justice. These words will issue from the judge, "Depart from me, ye cursed, into the everlasting fire which was prepared for the devil and his angels."[484]

But the elect will have a much different experience. The Holy Face to these is so gentle, so merciful and kind. They are glad to contemplate His Face, Him whose sufferings they were wont to meditate. "His wounds are as so many suns which inundate their souls with joy and happiness."[485] The degree of joy received on this last day will correspond to the degree each has attained in the different levels of the spiritual life. They shall hear the eternal lot: "Come ye blessed of My Father, possess you the

---

[481] See Matt. 24:30.

[482] Fourault, *The Month of the Holy Face*, p. 304.

[483] Ps. 103:32.

[484] Matt. 25:41.

[485] Fourault, *The Month of the Holy Face*, p. 307.

kingdom prepared for you from the foundation of the world."[486] They will be led by Jesus into the heavens. Saint Michael will take the cross from the heavens, and the procession will be ordered according to the degree of glory. The Blessed Virgin Mary will lead the martyrs and the virgins, followed by the confessors, bishops, priests, deacons, minor clerics, religious, married people, and the rest of elect humanity. At the end of the journey, they will be assigned different mansions, their eternal resting place; each mansion, with its degrees of beauty and size, will be given according to each one's degree of charity found in each soul at the moment they left time on earth.

### *Prayer of Blessed Pius IX*

O my Jesus! cast upon us a glance of mercy; turn Thy Face toward each one of us even as Thou didst towards Saint Veronica, not that we may see Thee with the eyes of our body, for we do not merit it, but turn it towards our hearts, so that, always remembering Thee, we may draw from this fountain of strength the vigor to sustain the necessary combats.[487]

## Transforming Union, Spiritual Marriage

The supreme development of the spiritual life follows. Souls in this state only want to talk to God or about God. Saint Dominic spoke only to God or of God and spent nights in front of the altar. Saint Thomas prayed for hours before the Blessed Sacrament at night.

---

[486] Matt. 25:34.

[487] Audience given to three parishes on Rome 10 March 1872.

> This holy joy of soul, the fruit of union with God may be desired, says St. Teresa,[488] whereas it is in no way fitting to desire visions and revelations, for they are extraordinary favors entirely distinct from the full development of the life of grace in our souls. St. Teresa declares: "know that for having received many favors of this kind, you will not merit more glory, but will be more stringently obliged to serve,[489] since you have received more. . . . There are many saints who never knew what it was to receive such favors, while others who have received them are not saints at all. . . . Indeed for one that is granted, the soul bears many a cross."[490]

What graces sometimes accompany transforming union? They may receive a ring, set with precious stones, like Blessed Alan de la Roche when the Blessed Virgin Mary asked him to promote the Confraternity of the Holy Rosary. They may hear celestial canticles of the angels, like Saint Francis, who went into ecstasy for over a day after hearing the first note. The Lord, the Blessed Virgin Mary, or the saints may appear to them. They may get an intellectual vision of the Holy Trinity. The soul still lives in faith, but its faith becomes singularly penetrating, luminous, and sweet.

Finally, we come to the study of the transforming union. Since it has progressed the former stages—painful mystical union, ecstatic union, and rapture—ecstasies cease as a rule,

---

[488] Teresa of Avila, *The Interior Castle*, 6th Mansion, ch. 9.

[489] Sr. Marie de St. Pierre was given the extraordinary gift of intellectual visions, but Jesus warned her that she would have to make an accounting of how she used these gifts.

[490] Teresa of Avila, *The Interior Castle,* 6th Mansion, ch. 9.

because, as Saint Teresa notes, the Lord has now strengthened, dilated, and developed the soul.[491] This eminent state is in no way miraculous because it is the perfect state of the spiritual life.[492] Saint John of the Cross explains that in transforming union, the higher faculties are drawn to the innermost center of the soul where the Blessed Trinity dwells. He continues, "The center of the soul is God . . . its ultimate and deepest center is God . . . the soul . . . enjoy[s] Him with all his strength."[493]

Using the analogy of the campfire, the soul is similar to white hot embers; the soul is thus completely consumed by the ardor of the Holy Spirit. At this stage, although the soul is in a state of spiritual perfection and the full development of grace, virtues, and the gifts are present, the soul may at times still be sorrowful unto death. Since devotion to the Passion is the gateway to transforming union, and devotion to the Holy Face is so linked to devotion to the Passion, consecration to the Holy Face can assist in bringing about transforming union, the prelude to the Beatific Vision.

The state of transforming union can be further explained theologically. Here, the soul is perfectly possessed of the gift of wisdom, the highest of the seven gifts received at Baptism. This union brings a great increase of sanctifying grace and charity. Holy souls wish Him to reign ever more profoundly in them, and God, in turn, is closer to them than the air they breathe is to their lungs.[494]

---

491 Teresa of Avila, *The Interior Castle,* 7th Mansion, ch. 3.

492 John of the Cross, *The Living Flame,* st. 2; A Spiritual Canticle, Part. III, st. 22ff.

493 John of the Cross, *The Living Flame,* st. I, v. 3.

494 *Summa Theologica* I–II, q. 28, a. 1, 2.

There are many levels of transforming union. Saint John of the Cross speaks of spiritual betrothals, in which a soul enjoys perfect union as a prelude and transitory way to transforming union.[495] In spiritual marriage, the highest union, the soul experiences union in a quasi-continual manner.

Some theologians consider transforming union equivalent to a special revelation, where some saints are told the date they will die and that they will be in heaven. But others say this cannot be certain as a theological rule.

Souls in transforming union have arrived at their deepest center, to which they were predestined, here on earth. This is the perfect realization of Christ's prayer, "That they be one, as we also are one: I in them and thou in me."[496]

What are the effects of transforming union? The soul is confirmed in grace.[497] That means they have a notable increase of divine love, because God removes occasions of sin and preserves it from mortal sin and almost always deliberate venial sin.

In spiritual marriage, God circumplexes the soul with intimacy, similar to the union between person united in marriage. There are no longer any secrets; there is a blending of two lives.[498] It sometimes can leave a wound or the stigmata. Those in this state have an ardent desire to be with God immediately and a burning desire to see the Holy Face of God in the Beatific Vision.

How does one receive this transforming union? Saint Teresa says, do not force it: "He dearly loves humility; if you think of yourselves unworthy to enter the third mansion, He will grant

---

[495] John of the Cross, *Spiritual Canticle*.

[496] John 17:22–23.

[497] Sp. Cant. st. 22.

[498] Tanquerey, Very Rev. Adolphe, *The Spiritual Life*, no. 1470.

you sooner the favor of entering the fifth."[499] Then you will be on your way to transforming union.

Some say that a very ardent desire for the Beatific Vision only exists once souls reach a certain level in the interior life. Members of the Confraternities of the Holy Face have an advantage, as the end of their devotion drives toward the Beatific Vision. Divine touches are present here because the soul has achieved complete detachment from everything created.[500]

Why is it that so few ever attain this state? The great work that God begins is thwarted because so many are too weak and run from trouble. They do not want to be mortified and kill sin. They want spiritual marriage sooner than the Holy Ghost wishes to grant it, and so they lack patience. The soul must pass through many tribulations and must have a great forgetfulness of self and a great desire to be immolated in imitation of Jesus Christ. Souls in transforming union are definitively marked with the image of Christ. Our Lord Jesus Christ promised Saint Gertrude[501] that those who honor the Holy Face "shall shine with a brightness surpassing that of many others in eternal life."

Souls need to make Communions more fervent each day and give adequate thanksgiving, even one hour a day immediately after receiving Holy Communion! They must never flee from trials which God sends them for their purification but face them like a soldier.

Last question: May generous persons who have seemed to pass through part of the night of the spirit ask for the grace of transforming union?

Certainly!

---

[499] Teresa of Avila, *The Interior Castle*, Epilogue.

[500] John of the Cross, *Dark Night of the Soul*, Bk. II, ch. 23.

[501] *Insinuations*, book iv, ch. vii.

Our Lady of the Holy Name of God, pray for us!

Now, turn to the prayers to be recited during the *unitive* way and the Chaplet of the Holy Face (p. 159, 20).

# Promises

## of Our Lord Jesus Christ in Favor of All Those Who Honor His Holy Face

1. They shall receive in themselves, by the impression of My humanity, a bright irradiation of My Divinity, and shall be so illuminated by it in their inmost souls, that, by their likeness to My Face, they shall shine with a brightness surpassing that of many others in eternal life (St. Gertrude, *Insinuations*, book IV, ch. vii).
2. Saint Mechtilde, having asked Our Lord that those who celebrate the memory of His sweet Face should never be deprived of His amiable company, He replied: "Not one of them shall be separated from Me" (Saint Mechtilde, *Of Spiritual Grace*, book I, ch. xiii).
3. "Our Lord," said Sister Marie de Saint-Pierre, "has promised me that He will imprint His divine likeness on the souls of those who honour His most holy countenance" (January 21, 1847). "This adorable Face is, as it were, the seal of the Divinity, which has the virtue of reproducing the likeness of God in the souls that are applied to it" (November 6, 1845).
4. "By My Holy Face you shall work miracles" (Our Lord to Sister Marie de Saint-Pierre, October 27, 1845).

5. "By My Holy Face you will obtain the conversion of many sinners. Nothing that you ask in making this offering will be refused to you. If you knew how pleasing the sight of My Face is to My Father!" (November 22, 1886).
6. "As in a kingdom you can procure all you wish for with a coin marked with the prince's effigy, so in the kingdom of Heaven you will obtain all you desire with the precious coin of My holy Humanity, which is My adorable countenance" (October 29, 1845).
7. "All those who honour My Holy Face in a spirit of reparation, will by so doing perform the office of the pious Veronica" (October 27, 1845).
8. "According to the care you take in making reparation to My Face disfigured by blasphemies, so will I take care of yours which has been disfigured by sin. I will reprint therein my image and render it as beautiful as it was on leaving the Baptismal font" (Our Lord to Sister Marie de Saint-Pierre, November 3, 1845).
9. "Our Lord has promised me," said again Sister Saint-Pierre, "for all those who defend His cause in this work of reparation, by words, by prayers, or writing, that He will defend them before His Father; at their death He will purify their souls by effacing all the blots of sin and will restore to them their primitive beauty" (March 12, 1846).

# Consecration Day (Day 34)

## The Consecration

At the end of thirty-three days, you should go to Confession and Communion, with the intention of giving yourself to Jesus and offering, in the hands of the Blessed Virgin Mary, His Holy Face to Our Heavenly Father for reparation for your sins and the sins of the world. At moment before receiving Holy Communion, ask the Holy Face of Jesus to help you make this Holy Communion the most fervent ever. Ask Him to help you to make exponentially more fervent Holy Communions and spiritual communions. Then you should recite the formula for consecration, according to the one as a member of the Archconfraternity of not a member. You ought to write it out or have it written, unless you have a printed copy of it; and you should sign it the same day on which you have made your consecration. You may have it signed by a witness, for example, a priest.

It would be well on that day to make some tribute to the Holy Face of Jesus, either as a penance for our past unfaithfulness to vows of Baptism, or as a testimony of dependence on the dominion of Jesus and Mary. This tribute should be one in accordance with your fervor, such as a fast, mortification or an alms, a candle, or erecting a shrine with the Holy Face of Jesus and establishing a lamp burning before It night and day.

Once a year at least, and on the same day, we should renew this consecration, observing some of the practices during the thirty-three days. It is a true gift to spontaneously be drawn by God throughout the day, and every day, to renew this consecration in one's own words.

## Act of Consecration to the Holy Face of Jesus

### Only For the Use of Members of the Archconfraternity

I, (n.), in order to give still greater increase to the glory of Jesus, dying for our salvation upon the cross, in order to correspond to the merciful love with which His Holy Face is animated towards poor sinners, and in order to repair the outrages which the frightful crimes of the present day inflict upon His august Face, the most pure mirror of the divine Majesty,—I associate myself, fully and freely, to the faithful received into this pious confraternity; I desire to participate in the indulgences with which it is enriched and in the good works practiced therein, as well for the expiation of my sins as for the solace of souls suffering in purgatory. Amiable Redeemer, most sweet Jesus, hide in the secret of Thy Face all the members of this association; may they there find shelter from the seductions of the world, and the snares of Satan; grant that, faithfully keeping all the precepts of Thy law and fulfilling the special duties of their state, they may be more and more inflamed with zeal for reparation, and with the flames of Thy divine love. Amen.

# Act of Consecration of Ourselves to the Holy Face of Jesus

## For Non-members

O adorable Face of my Jesus, humbly prostrate in Thy divine presence, I desire to consecrate myself wholly to Thee and henceforth to live only for Thee. Why have I not at my disposal the hearts of all creatures, in order to offer them up as a holocaust to Thee? Alas, O well beloved Face, I have only my own, unworthy as it is of Thy attention and often rebelling against the movements of Thy grace; nevertheless, I give it to Thee, my poor heart, and I consecrate it to Thee, in order that, from this moment and during all the days of my life, it may be inflamed with the holy ardor of Thy divine love. Purify it, warm it with the blessed rays of Thy eternal light, so that I may henceforth exclaim with the prophet king: "Lord, the light of Thy Face is engraved upon us; Thou hast caused joy to spring forth in my heart" (Ps. 4:7).

I offer Thee then this day, deliberately and with great joy, the sacrifice of all the delights which may be offered me on earth. Accept, O adorable Face, O Thou whom I love more than aught else in the world, accept the homage of myself, which I present to Thee at this moment. I thrill with gladness and with love, whilst thus consecrating to Thee the whole of my being. Yes, I offer and consecrate to Thee my heart, my body, my soul, my spirit, and my life; my heart, to love only Thee, O beauty ever ancient and ever new; my body, to serve as an instrument of reparation and of all that belongs to Thy glory; my soul, to reflect unceasingly the image of Thy different graces; my spirit, to think only upon thee, and upon all that will tend to spread devotion to Thee; my life, my whole life, in order that it may be penetrated with Thy sweet memory, and filled with actions worth Thy Name, so that I may one day merit that life eternal, in which, according to the expression of Thy apostle, I may contemplate Thee, no longer as in an enigma and through a mirror, but face to face, and as Thou art.

Whilst waiting until this supreme grace shall be accorded to me, O Holy Face of Jesus, make me walk here below in the light of Thy benign eyes, that when I shall appear before Thee, Thou mayest name me by my name, Thou mayest kiss me with the kiss of Thy mouth, and Thou mayest introduce me into the immortal society of the blessed who are occupied without ceasing in contemplating Thee, praising Thee, adoring Thee, and eternally singing Thy mercies. Amen.

# Bibliography


Agreda, Mary of Jesus. *Mystical City of God*. Washington, NJ: Blue Army of Our Lady of Fatima, 1996. 4 volumes.

Albert the Great. *The Paradise of the Soul: Forty-Two Virtues to Reach Heaven*. Gastonia, NC: TAN Publishers, 2023.

Alphonsus de Liguori. *Preparation for Death*. Brooklyn: Redemptorist Fathers, 1934.

———. *The Holy Eucharist*. Brooklyn: Redemptorist Fathers, 1934.

———. *The Passion and the Death of Jesus Christ*. Brooklyn: Redemptorist Fathers, 1927.

Aquinas, Thomas. *De poenitentia.*

———. *Summa Theologica.*

Arnoudt, Peter. *Imittion of the Sacred Heart of Jesus*. Charlotte, North Carolina; TAN Books; 2011.

Augustine. *De civitate Dei contra paganos.*

Bergamo, Padre Gaetano Maria. *Humility of Heart.* Mandeville, LA, 2017.

Bernard of Clairvaux. *De gradibus humilitatis.*

Bocquet, Marcel. *The Firebrand.* Washington, DC: Corda Press, 1966.

Catherine of Siena, *Dialogues.* London; Kegan Paul, Trench, Trubner & Co., Ltd.; 1896.

Chautard, Dom Jean-Baptiste. *The Soul of the Apostolae.* Rockford, IL: TAN Publishers, 1974.

Forbes, F. A. *St. Catherine of Siena.* Charlotte, North Carolina; TAN Books; 1998.

Fourault, J. B. *The Month of the Holy Face.* Tours: Oratory of the Holy Face, 1891.

Francis de Sales. *Treatise on the Love of God.* Rockford, IL: TAN Publishers, 1988.

———. *The Introduction to the Devout Life.* Gastonia, NC: TAN Publishers, 2023.

Gabriel of St. Mary Magdalen. *Divine Intimacy*. Rockford, IL: TAN Publishers, 1996.

Garrigou-Lagrange, Reginald. *Three Ages of the Interior Life.* 2 Volumes. Rockford, IL: TAN Publishers, 1989.

———. *The Three Conversions in the Spiritual Life.* Rockford, IL: TAN Publishers, 2002.

Janvier, Abbé. *Life of Sister Mary St. Peter Carmelite of Tours.* Palissy, Tours, France: The Oratory of the Holy Face, 1884.

———. *Manual of the Archconfraternity of the Holy Face.* Palissy, Tours, France: The Oratory of the Holy Face, 1887.

John of the Cross. *Ascent of Mount Carmel.* Garden City, NY: Image Books, 1958.

———. *Dark Night of the Soul.* London; Thomas Baker; 1908.

———. *Spiritual Canticle.* Garden City, New York; Image Books; 1961.

Kevin, Father O.C.D. *Way of Perfection for the Laity: A Detailed Explanation of the Discalced Carmelite Third Secular Order Rule*. Dublin: Gill, 1956.

Lallement, Charles. *La Doctrine spirituelle.* Paris, 1908.

L'Espirit de Sainte Thérèse de l' Enfant Jésus.

Louis de Montfort. *True Devotion to Mary*. Rockford, IL: TAN Publishers, 1985.

———. *The Secret of the Rosary*. Bay Shore, NY: Montfort Publications, 1990.

Marmion, Columba. *Christ in His Mysteries*. London; Sands; 1931.

———. *Christ the Life of the Soul.* Tacoma WA; Angelico Press; 2021.

Müller, Fr. Michael, C.SS.R. *The Holy Sacrafice of the Mass.* Rockford, IL: TAN Books and Publishers, 1992.

Pereira, Fr. Manual Sousa. *The Admirable Life of Mother Mriana.* Los Angeles, CA: Tradition in Action, 2020.

Ripperger, Chad. *The Binding Force of Tradition*. Sensus Traditionis Press, 2013.

Scallan, Dorothy. *The Holy Man of Tours: Apostle of the Holy Face Devotion (1797-1876)*. Rockford, IL: TAN Books and Publishers, 1990.

———. *The Golden Arrow: The Revelations of Sr. Mary of St. Peter*. Rockford, IL: TAN Books and Publishers, 1990.

———. *The Whole World Will Love Me: The Life of St. Thérèse of the Child Jesus and of the Holy Face*. Rockford, IL: TAN Books and Publishers, 2005.

Sheed, F. J. *Communism and Man*. London: Purnell, 1938.

Sheen, Fulton, J. *The Cross and the Crib*. Midland, Ontario: Bishop Sheen Today Publishing, 2021.

Tanquerey, The Very Reverend Adolphe, S. S., D.D. *The Spiritual Life: A Treatise on Ascetical and Mystical Theology.* Charlotte, NC: TAN Publishers, 2000.

Thérèse. *The Story of a Soul.* Charlotte, NC: TAN Publishers, 2012.

Teresa of Avila, *Life.* Garden City, New York; Image Books; 1960.

———. *The Way of Perfection*. Charlotte, NC: TAN Publishers, 2011.

———. *The Interior Castle*. Charlotte, NC: TAN Publishers, 2011.

Thomas à Kempis. *Imitation of Christ*. Brooklyn, NY: Confraternity of the Precious Blood, 1982.

Verheylezoon, Louis. *Devotion to the Sacred Heart*. Rockford, IL: TAN Publishers, 1978.

Varano, Camilla Battisa. *Life and Writings: From Worldly Princess to the Foot of the Cross.* Icona Press, 2022.